No Broom Re

Astral travel is already part of your psy
every night in your dreams. In order to ~~be able~~ to remember and
consciously direct your astral travels, you need to possess the
tools and techniques that will take you safely to the astral planes
and bring you back again.

Flying Without a Broom clearly details basic and advanced methods for traveling the astral, through altered states of consciousness such as meditation and sleep. Visit the astral planes to work
magick and healings; contact teachers, guides, or lovers; and
build psychic defenses for yourself, your home, and your family.
You can even view Akashic records of your former lives to recognize past mistakes and negative relationships that may be causing you trouble today. You'll also find out how to protect yourself
and others from the low-level entities encountered in the astral.

Flying Without a Broom far exceeds the scope of most books on
astral projection. From tips on remembering your journeys to
how-to's for uncovering valuable knowledge in the astral realms,
D. J. Conway makes this exciting practice accessible to you—no
broom required!

About the Author

I was born on a Beltane Full Moon with a total lunar eclipse, one of the hottest days of that year. Although I came into an Irish-North Germanic-Native American family with natural psychics on both sides, such abilities were not talked about. So I learned discrimination in a family of closet psychics.

I have always been close to Nature. As a child, I spent a great amount of time outdoors by myself. Trees, herbs, and flowers become part of my indoor and outdoor landscapes wherever I live. I love cats, music, mountains, singing streams, stones, ritual, nights when the Moon is full. My reading covers vast areas of history, the magickal arts, philosophy, customs, mythology, and fantasy. I have studied every part of the New Age religions from Eastern philosophy to Wicca. I hope I never stop learning and expanding.

Although I have lived in areas of this country from one coast to the other, I now reside on the West Coast. I am not fond of large crowds or speaking in public.

I live a rather quiet life in the company of my husband and my four cats, with occasional visits with my children and grandchildren. I collect statues of dragons and wizards, crystals and other stones, and of course, books. Most of my time is spent researching and writing. My published books include *Celtic Magic; Norse Magic; The Ancient & Shining Ones; Maiden, Mother, Crone; Dancing With Dragons; Animal Magick;* and *Moon Magick.* Before I am finished with one book, I am working on another in my head. All in all, I am just an ordinary Pagan person.

To Write to the Author

If you wish to contact the author or would like more information about this book, please write to the author in care of Llewellyn Worldwide, and we will forward your request. Both the author and the publisher appreciate hearing from you and learning of your enjoyment of this book and how it has helped you. Llewellyn Worldwide cannot guarantee that every letter written to the author can be answered, but all will be forwarded. Please write to:

D. J. Conway
℅ Llewellyn Worldwide
P.O. Box 64383-K164, St. Paul, MN 55164-0383, U.S.A.
Please enclose a self-addressed, stamped envelope or $1.00 to cover costs.
If outside the U.S.A., enclose international postal reply coupon.

Free Catalog from Llewellyn

Flying Without a Broom

Astral Projection and the Astral World

D. J. Conway

1995
Llewellyn Publications
St. Paul, MN 55164-0383, U.S.A.

FIRST EDITION
Second Printing, 1995

Cover painting: Helen Nelson-Reed
Cover design: Tom Grewe
Illustrations: Tom Grewe
Book design, layout, and editing: Jessica Thoreson

Library of Congress Cataloging-in-Publication Data
Conway, D. J. (Deanna J.)
        Flying without a broom: astral projection and the astral
        world / D. J. Conway. — 1st ed.
            p.   cm.
        Includes bibliographical references and index.
        ISBN 1-56718-164-3 (trade pbk.)
        1. Astral projection. I. Title.
BF1389.A7C66   1995
133.9—dc20   95-16124
                                                              CIP

Printed in the United States of America

Llewellyn Publications
A Division of Llewellyn Worldwide, Ltd.
P.O. Box 64383, St. Paul, MN 55164-0383

Table of Contents

One

Astral Projection and History

Many of the old stories tell of witches flying across the night sky on brooms on the way to their gatherings. The old woman with her broom even has a part in children's nursery rhymes. Most of the recorded "evidence" was not of actual sightings, but rather that people had heard of such flights. Sounds wonderful, doesn't it? Just take out the broom and go wherever you want. Well, I can tell you how to fly without a broom. It's called astral projection and travel, and it is really not that difficult to learn.

Astral projection and travel is no more dangerous or difficult than driving a car. When you learn the basics, obey the rules, and show appropriate concern for both yourself and others, you can easily get where you want to go.

Almost everyone in these times is familiar with the term "astral travel" or "astral projection." Some don't believe in it because they don't believe in the astral body. However, many more people do believe in astral travel, either through their cultural teachings or personal experience.

Astral travel and/or projection is accomplished by the astral body leaving the physical body and going to other places or times. In some mystical teachings, this astral form is called the light and/or the emotional body.

Some writers say that you have to be able to look at your physical body from the outside for you to be actually astral traveling. However, this isn't necessarily true. Have you experienced dreams of falling, flying, or gliding? Have you been awakened because you felt as if something or someone had slammed your body hard? Have you awakened because someone called your name, but found no physical person had done so? Have you been so deep in meditation or "daydreaming" that you had no sense of the physical body? If you have experienced any of these situations, you were astral traveling.

Everyone dreams, even if they can't remember. There are certain categories of dreams that are not dreams at all, but remembrances of astral traveling. Participating in dream action, as opposed to just watching the action, especially if the colors are very vivid, is a signal of astral projection. Have you had dreams of the future, visiting deceased loved ones, or reliving very vivid scenes from history? You have been astral traveling through time and space.

History and mythology are full of examples of the astral body visiting other places and other times. The ideas of the astral body and its ability to transcend and move through time and space were known as far back as ancient Egypt, Greece, and Mesopotamia, if not earlier. The Hindus and the Norse knew of it. The same magickal powers were credited to yogins, fakirs, and alchemists.

It is very likely that astral travel began to be explored in a spiritual and practical sense during the time of the matriarchal cultures. This flying ability was attributed to all humans during the mythological period of many civilizations. This talent was still a part of Goddess Mysteries during later periods of history. Goddess and matriarchal connections may well have been a reason why the Christians went after witches and Pagans in such a destructive way.

Many people believe that the notorious witch trials happened during the Dark Ages, but this isn't true. Although there were isolated witch trials during this period of history, the most vicious and concentrated of them took place between the fifteenth and eighteenth centuries.

One of the most prominent features of the witch trials were the "confessions" tortured from women about flying on a broom, staff, or animal familiar to a Sabbat meeting where they frolicked with demons (old Pagan deities). Fantastic as it seems, people really believed that these women had gone physically flying through the night. One recorded testimony from the 1600s tells of a woman named Julian Cox who was out walking early one evening. Coming toward her on broomsticks were three people a full yard off the ground. More than one man told of seeing his mother-in-law fly up the chimney on her broom. One wonders if Ms. Cox hadn't been sipping bad ale and the sons-in-law just wanted rid of their wives' mothers.

As the witch trials grew more frenzied, more and more people (particularly women) were accused by those who wanted their property or just to be rid of them. The flying reports became more ridiculous and outrageous. Technically, physical flying in such a manner is not impossible if one could learn to correctly apply the rules of magick, but this knowledge was no longer available to these uneducated people. Even today the knowledge remains lost.

A great many of these witch confessions tell of using an ointment compounded of dangerous plants to help with this. As far back as the ancient book *The Golden Ass* by Apuleius, there is mention of flying ointments. None of the translations of the ingredients can be called accurate, and they all contain deadly plants. Many of the ingredients, such as bat's blood and children's fat, were included to confuse the uninitiated. Several of the plants will cause rapid heartbeat and delusions, if they don't kill you.

3

Obviously, these drugs were used to help the witch astral travel because she had forgotten, or never known, how to astral travel otherwise. The single greatest problem with drug-induced astral travel is that one has little or no control, which could account for some of the strange reports given by the witches.

It is quite unnecessary, and very dangerous, to use drugs to produce a loosening of the astral body from the physical body. You want your mind to be totally under your control during meditation and/or astral travel. Besides, the brain produces its own chemicals for a "high." It was discovered in 1959 that the pineal gland secretes melatonin, which is derived from serotonin, similar in molecular structure to LSD. Other studies found that the brain also produces dimethyltryptamine, another conscious-ness-altering drug. Both these chemicals are secreted by the brain during periods of relaxed visualization.

In 1647, Henry More, a Christian and student of occult phi-losophy, wrote that these witches were traveling in their astral forms, not their physical bodies. It's a wonder the man wasn't tortured and burned alive for such a statement. The Church and the authorities, however, simply used his words to further justify their purges. This persecution extended to anyone who spoke of traveling astrally, even if they didn't believe or participate in Witchcraft. It was a common saying during that period that witches and wizards cast no shadows; astral bodies don't cast shadows, either, which automatically made any astral traveler a witch. After all, such behavior and obvious practice of Paganism wasn't sanctioned by the Church, and couldn't be claimed as god-given since Pagans used it. Therefore, these misguided souls should be tortured and killed for their own good. Unfortunately, there are still people with this type of mentality today.

Dame Alice Kyteler was the first witch formally tried by the Church for flying. During her trial in 1324, Alice spoke of her staff by which she galloped through "thick and thin." Later writ-ers have said that "thick and thin" meant she rode the staff on the ground like a hobby horse, which fits with other reports of the time. However, this expression also describes astral travel through the layers of the Otherworlds. Since she greased the staff with flying ointment, Alice may have done both the physical riding on the ground and astral traveling with her astral body.

The detailed Church prohibition against witches started soon after this. The Council of Constance, held from 1414 to 1418, concocted a long list of offenses by which one could identify a witch. They also applied the same rules to any practitioner of black magick. Strangely enough, astral flying was not on the list. These crusaders-against-Pagans apparently were not aware of this ability. As soon as the Church found out more about it, though, astral flying was added to the list.

Shamans the world over have always known about astral travel. It is an important part of their ceremonies and rituals. Shamanism is not limited to the Native Americans of the Western Hemisphere and the Eskimos and Lapps. At one time, shamanic practices were used throughout Europe and the Mediterranean area. The shaman speaks of riding her/his staff or horse on a mystical journey to gather information. This horse traveled through the air to distant places or through time. Many times these "horses" were described as having eight legs, which reminds one of the Norse god Odhinn's horse, Sleipnir. The horse was often symbolized by the burning of white horsehairs or the shaman sitting on a white mare's skin.

This symbolism of magickal flight extended beyond the bounds of shamanism and Witchcraft into the field of universal magick. It played an essential part in a great many religious practices before and after the evolution of shamanism and Witchcraft. Stories tell of the magician reaching the flying state by climbing a ladder, tree, or tent pole where she/he turned into a bird, mounted a flying horse, rode an arrow, or other similar conveyances.

The Mithraic religion spoke of a ladder (*klimax*) with seven rungs which enabled the initiate to climb to the heavens. Siberian shamans used a tent pole or tree with seven or nine notches. Mohammed and Jacob saw stairs reaching to "heaven." The later Christian Saints spoke of seven-stepped stairs leading to heaven. Part of the Greek Orphic tradition called for the initiate to climb a ladder to the sky world.

Followers of the Greek god Apollo experienced astral travel as seen in the story of Abaris, who was said to fly through the air on a golden arrow given to him by Apollo. Apollo was said to have come from the country of the Hyperboreans in the north, who probably had shamanic traditions.

Plato, in his *Republic,* wrote of a man who was supposedly killed on the battlefield and returned to life twelve days later as they laid him on the funeral pyre. This man, Er the Pamphylian, spoke of flying about and seeing the world of the gods.

In India, ancient texts speak of the importance of magickal flight to the development of the soul. Spiritual ascent by "climbing a tree" is mentioned in the Brahmanic scriptures. Buddha took seven steps and saw all over the world. Among certain non-Aryan people of India, the magician still dances himself into ecstasy using a horse-headed stick. The Rig Veda tells how priests and/or magicians can recover a lost or wandering soul by "flying" into other realms of being. This doctrine of the wandering (or astral traveling) soul is still applied in the Hindu belief where they say a sleeping person should not be awakened suddenly.

Although the broomstick is the most common item mentioned for astral flying by witches, it was only one of the possible "steeds" used. The broom of those times had no resemblance to what we call a broom today. It had a stout central pole, around one end of which were tied bunches of broom (*Planta genista* or *genet),* birch twigs, or heather. The broom (bossume, bossom, or besom) was an ordinary implement used by a woman; the equivalent for a man would have been the pitchfork. The Christians turned the broom-riding female witch into a wicked old hag and the pitchfork-riding male witch into a devil.

The Celtic people of Scotland said that the witch flew on a bune wand. Sometimes this was described as a forked stick and other times as merely a staff. In fact, a bune wand came to mean anything that a witch used to ride on, including stems and stalks of plants.

The mystical and sexual magick of the broomstick has come down to us today hidden in the form of nursery rhymes and toys. For example, hobby horses (sticks with horse-heads) are still ridden by small children. Fortunately, sexually repressed parents have no idea what the original meaning was. In the old traditions, the broomstick symbolized the sacred sexual unions between the Pagan God and Goddess.

Take a look at one old nursery rhyme:

> *Ride a cock-horse to Banbury Cross*
> *To see a fine lady upon a white horse.*
> *With rings on her fingers and bells on her toes,*
> *She shall have music wherever she goes.*

This is full of hidden sexual and sacred symbolism. The white horse was the consort of the Goddess, or his representative in the physical, with the cock-horse symbolizing a penis. The fine lady was the Goddess, or Her physical representative. The lady riding the cock-horse is a metaphor for the woman on top during intercourse, a position forbidden by the Christian leaders. To the Pagans, this position symbolized the magickal power of women, and the priestess in particular. To the Christians, this meant a loss of control and power to males. The sacred union, called the *hieros gamos* by the Greeks, in this position was used to call up vast quantities of magickal power for a specific purpose. Originally, this sexual union was not a frivolous activity, although it may have degenerated into open sexual free-for-all gatherings later when much of the old knowledge was lost.

Sufi mystics of the Middle Ages rode horse-headed canes called *zamalzain* (gala limping horses) in their ecstatic dances. They also had groups of thirteen members, containing six men and six women, with the thirteenth member being a man who represented the Rabba or Lord.

Banbury Cross was the crossroads, a potent place for the holding of rituals recorded as far back as the worship of Hecate. The rings on Her fingers were symbols of prosperity and blessing, while the bells on Her toes represented the music for the sacred dances. Whatever the Goddess touched or wherever She walked were considered to be blessed; the same applied to Her priestesses. The hands and feet are a reference to the power centers in the palms and soles.

Another nursery rhyme:

There was an old woman tossed up in a basket.
Up she sailed as high as the Moon.
Where she was going, I couldn't but ask her,
For in her hand she carried a broom.
Old woman, old woman, old woman, said I.
Oh whither, oh whither, oh whither so high?
To brush the cobwebs out of the sky.

Baskets and brooms have been sacred symbols as long as there has been recorded history. In this case, the basket and broom represent the "steed" for astral travel for the old woman (witch or priestess) as she sails to the Moon (a powerful source of magickal energy). The number three is a sacred number, often connected with the Triple Goddess. Rituals and spells repeated three times are said to have great potency; thus the thrice repeated words to the old woman may be a reference to a forgotten ritual which could help induce astral travel. Sweeping cobwebs out of the sky symbolizes magickal work on the astral plane which will eventually take form in the physical.

History and mythology are full of references to astral projection and travel. It is nothing new to humans. At one time, astral travel was considered a vital and necessary part of spiritual development, especially for initiates. Unfortunately, most people today fear it as something evil. Astral projection and travel are part of your psychic make-up, whether you like it or not. You do it every night, even though you might not remember your travels.

Since astral travel is such an integrated part of your being, why not learn to remember and actively participate in it? Regardless of what you may have been told, traveling in this manner is not difficult. It just takes a little practice, determination, and a sense of anticipation. And you don't need a broom!

Two

The Astral Plane

One of the first things to understand about astral travel has to be the divisions of your mind which influence it. The brain is not the same as the mind; the brain is a physical body organ, while the mind, which comes from the Greek word *menos* (spirit), is the part of an individual which feels, perceives, thinks, remembers, and wills. Although scientists have determined many functions of the brain, science doesn't have any idea or explanation for the function of the mind (except in vague terms), or even where it is possibly located.

The conscious mind is the most active in humans, for it is associated with the dominant left brain. It maintains control over thoughts, solves problems in what it determines to be a logical manner, works with language and mathematics, and deals totally with what it perceives to be reality. The fast, low-voltage brainwaves of 14-28 cycles per second connected with activity in the conscious mind are called Beta waves. Beta waves can spike above 50 cycles when you are under stress, such as when you are experiencing fear, anxiety, frustration, or anger.

The subconscious mind is associated with the creative right brain. It is artistic, intuitive, visualizing, and deals with what we call imagination and creativity. It is the powerful belief formed in this area of the mind that creates manifestations and enables one to work magick. The subconscious mind exhibits Alpha brainwaves of 8-13 cycles per second. Often these Alpha waves are mixed with still slower Theta waves during periods of contemplation. The subconscious mind has ten times the power of the conscious mind when it is in the Alpha-Theta state; this enables it to perform "impossible" feats. This mixture of Alpha-Theta waves appears to be common even during non-meditation activities by creative and psychic people.

There is a third part of the mind that is given little attention by most people. This is the superconscious mind, the most nebulous part of our thinking process. It is this section that emits the drowsy state of the Theta waves, which are 4-7 cycles per second. When we successfully reach the superconscious mind state, we are in deep meditation, trance, or astral traveling. It is through the superconscious mind that humans establish communication with deities, teachers, and guides, or other such entities.

There is a fourth category of brainwaves called the Delta. These are extremely slow, from 0.5-3 cycles per second. The Delta state is associated with part of the superconscious mind, but these waves are only exhibited during the deepest cycles of sleep.

Most people work with only 10 percent of their potential. That's all that can be reached through use of the Beta waves, or conscious mind. The other 90 percent can only be tapped by going deeper into the Alpha-Theta areas. An altered state of consciousness (which means deep meditation and/or astral travel) is the only way to reach these areas. Once we accept that the visualizations we are seeing are not our "imagination," the nervous system of our being experiences them.

This altered state of consciousness does a strange and wonderful thing—in the physical body, the nerve endings, which are usually disassociated to a lesser or greater degree, come together. The dendrites and axones of the nerves link up until our nervous system works smoothly and more effectively without any strain. This has been proven in cases of senility due to old age. Once an older person begins to be truly interested in something again, feels useful and productive, and begins to use her/his creative abilities, the person becomes less senile.

However, there are certain people who should not engage in deliberate astral travel. Several respected writers in such areas as metaphysics, bio-feedback, and psychiatry give the same warnings: depressive neurotics, those with dangerously overactive imaginations, epileptics, mental patients, heavy marijuana users, and hard drug addicts should not engage in deep meditation, trance, deliberate astral traveling, or bio-feedback training. These problems frequently get worse in these people.

The same applies if a person is unstable in any way, highly open to suggestion, or unwilling to face the truth of her/his actions and life. Many commercial mind-training teachers are actually incompetent in working with people and end up doing more harm than good. They are not aware of individual personalities and needs; they are concerned only with disseminating information to a large group without a checks and balances system. If you are sincere in your desires and efforts, and have no serious physical problems (such as heart trouble—deliberate astral projection alters the heartbeat and respiration) or mental disorders, you don't need to pay hundreds or thousands of dollars for a mind-training course. You can do it yourself at your own speed and geared to your own personal spiritual beliefs. This way, you know who is in control—you!

When learning to understand astral projection and travel, you must accept the fact that you are working directly with your subconscious and, through it, the superconscious mind. You can't reach the superconscious mind without going through the subconscious. The conscious mind won't even acknowledge that either of the others exists. So we give the conscious mind something to do that it understands (such as meditation, ritual, or relaxation techniques) while we slip through into the greater and more productive areas of the mind.

All traditions which believe in the astral plane say that there is more than one level to it. Several traditions state that there are seven levels, with higher and lower areas for departed souls and other entities. It is possible that these levels are connected in some way with the seven major chakra or light centers in the astral body.

These astral planes are not totally separated from one another, except for the very highest plane, which is actually above the seven levels. Each of the seven levels gently merges into the one above it, rather like the colors of a rainbow merge into each other.

Witches, Pagans, ceremonial magicians, and shamans believe that the astral plane is made up of spirits, both human and elemental. This Otherworld realm is made up of a different type of energy that vibrates at a higher and much different rate than this physical world. The astral plane and this world surround and interpenetrate each other. That is why when you astral travel, you are able to tap into what is happening in this world as well as in the astral.

No one can travel astrally (or any other way) to the very highest level above the seven astral levels. The vibrations of this area are so refined that only the Supreme Creative Power and the very few attendant beings who answer only to Her/Him/It can enter that level. These attendant beings (angels, special high masters) come and go from there, carrying messages and instructions from this Power and carrying out Her/His/Its wishes. This Supreme Creative Power is the God behind the Gods.

Directly below this is the seventh astral level, the plane or area of the deity archetypes, entities we might call the Gods. With the proper spiritual (not religious) preparation and resolve, it is possible for you to visit this level. Entities from this astral level can also bring you up to them, or come down to you. It is through their abilities, power, and caring that humans re-learn the ancient wisdoms. By gaining their assistance in magickal workings, you can create a manifestation of a desired end on the physical plane.

At the other end of the vibrational spectrum is the lowest level. This is basically an area of spiritual darkness, a place of malevolent thoughtforms, earthbound spirits, and devolved human souls. Some souls are there simply because they believe they must suffer in the orthodox hell; others because their vibrations are so dense that they cannot progress, and do not want to progress, upward.

Those souls who are there by choice through erroneous thinking can leave for higher levels as soon as they understand that their "hell" is not real, but self-created. The eons-old tradition of praying for the souls of ancestors or the dead has a mystical reason behind it. The dead can be aware of the living if they choose; prayers for those who trap themselves on this level can eventually convince them that they are free to move into higher vibrations.

The malicious spirits of this lowest of astral levels are the ones who haunt buildings or areas of nature; sometimes they will try to harm humans. They are inherently evil and nothing can be done for them, except remove them (if possible) from their haunting area and confine them to their astral level. This type of removing action takes a dedicated, trained, and powerful magician or exorcist. Even then it can be a frightening and draining procedure. If such a spirit gains entrance to a human body, it is vastly more difficult to remove and return to its astral plane. This is because the human must in some way agree to be "possessed" in the first place.

Early in my magickal studies, I ran into both types of evil entity hauntings, and both were hair-raising experiences. The first experience had to do with a ghost in a house, the second was a possession.

My children and I moved into an old house in the country, primarily because the rent was all I could afford. I found out later why it was so cheap. This house had two stairways to the upstairs section. One set of stairs was quite normal; the other was ice cold, even in the hottest summer. My oldest daughter was a sensitive, budding psychic and began to have nightmares from the day we moved in. Although the cold stairway was next to her room, she used the other one. The other two children also didn't like that stairway; even their friends avoided it. Whenever anyone (including non-believing guests) went down it, there was a heavy, evil feeling that followed them all the way to the bottom. Those who used it expected to be pushed down the stairs at any time. We discovered that fifty years earlier a sixteen-year-old boy died in the room at the top of that stairway; he had been a malicious bully.

This spirit became such a bad mental influence and created so many psychic disturbances that finally I had to do an exorcism. We thought he was gone, but that night the upper windows began to rattle. We could hear the noise clearly downstairs. Deciding there was strength in numbers, we all went upstairs and opened a window. A gust of cold air shot past us and out the window. End of story? No, because at night we could see the spirit sitting in a tree outside the windows. We moved shortly afterward. I don't think you could have totally gotten rid of him unless you burned down the house.

The second experience proved two things to me: first, you exorcise a spirit through what it believes, not what you believe; and second, a possessing spirit needs the consent of the person being possessed.

I had a friend at that time whose lifestyle didn't quite fit with mine, but as a friend he was good company. Jerry had led a rather "colorful" life in Los Angeles before he moved back to Oregon. One day he received news that a close friend of his had been murdered in a drug deal. Jerry decided, unbeknownst to me, to contact this deceased friend and allow him to possess his body. When he showed up at my door one evening, I sensed immediately that something was wrong. The voice, the mannerisms, everything was totally different. This possessing spirit wasn't the least bit shy about admitting what had happened; in fact, he bragged about it.

There I was, alone, with a possessed person who threatened my life if I called anyone to help. I knew the police weren't about to believe me, but I also knew I needed help. As soon as Jerry went off to use the bathroom, I grabbed the phone and dialed a local husband and wife team who had a metaphysical-Christian church. They arrived shortly, and there ensued a verbal battle complete with threats from the entity.

The wife kept trying to run him out by calling on Jesus. The entity just laughed; he didn't believe in Jesus. Finally, the husband and I decided to visualize throwing fire on him through our hands. This the spirit understood. He started screaming, "You're burning me!" We informed him his only option was to leave, which he immediately did.

This is not to say that an exorcism can be this easy; the few I've heard about haven't been. But one must use what a possessing spirit believes in. It's rather like the old joke about the Jewish vampire faced by his victim holding a cross—the victim was bitten anyway.

Fortunately, most of the spirits which inhabit the lower astral plane don't have the power or invitation necessary for them to cause humans on this physical plane any trouble. Cases of vicious hauntings or possessions are rare. The ways to avoid them, either while in your physical body or while astral traveling, is to keep high ethical morals, seek true spiritual enlightenment, accept responsibility for what you do and say, and make an honest effort to learn about your past lives in order to overcome karmic problems. After all, like attracts like.

The five intermediate astral levels range from what might be termed beginning to the advanced. These are the astral levels you want to actively seek in your travel. The only way you will be able to travel to the higher levels is if your spiritual thoughts match the vibration there, and if you are not harboring negative emotions.

Here you can receive guidance from and communicate with your teachers, visit with other astral travelers or deceased loved ones, discover ancient mystical knowledge, and perform some of your most powerful spellworkings. These astral levels are the ones you should have as a definite goal when you go into meditation or plan astral travel. You will not be threatened on these levels, but can expect to be protected and guided to the exact place, class, or teacher that will help you most.

The souls of nature spirits, animals, and beings created by many strongly projected human thoughts dwell in certain areas. The created thoughtforms which are negative and malicious are confined to the first, or lowest, level. Other more productive, positive thoughtforms can be within any of the five intermediate levels. Nature spirits are usually on the second astral level, while the souls of animals, depending upon their development, can also be on any of the middle areas.

If you think this idea of living thoughtforms is far-fetched, think again. Thoughts have energy; the electrical impulses (thoughts) of the brain, whose connection with the mind we do not entirely understand, are a form of energy. Every time you think or visualize, you are putting out energy pulses. The same thoughts or ideals held by many people will eventually create a corresponding entity in the astral. This is seen in ancient sacred stones, worship areas or buildings, and statues. The image ideal has become a living creature on the astral, sending its power through the sacred object. Sometimes, as with the orthodox "Devil," the thoughtform is so strong that it does not need an object to make its power felt. However, you must believe in this entity for it to have power over you.

The astral plane is sensitive to thoughts and emotions. All thoughts are triggered by emotions, some weak, some powerful. All thoughtforms must be created by an emotion—fear, anger, hate, love, desire, intense spirituality—that is the only way a thoughtform can come into existence. This is expressed in the old saying, "That which you fear most will happen." This is because constantly fearing something provides a steady stream of energy, thus creating, or adding to, a thoughtform. Denying your fear, if you still actually fear it, is not getting rid of the energy flow. You have to replace the negative thought with a positive one. For example, if you believe in reincarnation, there is no longer any reason to fear death.

Wendell was new to Pagan practices and still trying to clean out old orthodox religious ideas. When he began to go out onto the astral in meditation, he ran into what he described as "the Devil" on one of his astral excursions. The very sight of this entity popped him right back into his physical body. The entity was quite real on the astral and gave off feelings of evil and danger.

Wendell thought about this malevolent entity, decided he didn't believe in it, and went back to the astral. "The Devil" showed up again. This time Wendell was ready for him. "I don't believe in you," he said. "What's more, I don't want you around." He traced a glowing pentagram in the air between him and the entity. "Get lost," he ordered. "Go find somebody who is afraid of you." The entity made a few futile grabbing gestures, then disappeared. "That entity was somebody else's program," Wendell told me. "I just decided I wouldn't accept it anymore."

Part of the astral world is the world of what we call ghosts, or positive earthbound spirits. This is on one of the lower astral levels. If you want to contact deceased people who don't hang around negatively haunting people or places, you have to go above the first astral level. There are positive earthbound spirits who stay around places and people they loved when they had a physical body. Our present home came with a little old lady; she has never been any trouble.

The more advanced souls exist in surroundings they create to reflect their ideas of an afterlife. Some continue to stay in these surroundings until they reincarnate, while others learn quickly that they don't have to stay in a preconceived religious atmosphere of life after death. It's very interesting to visit with these souls, especially if they are some of your ancestors. You can find out about family history and everyday life during the times they lived on Earth.

There is an old saying, "As above, so below." There are two ways of interpreting this; both are correct. First, that what exists in the astral-spiritual realms is repeated on this Earth plane. We know that there are good and bad people who inhabit this existence. Therefore, there are good and bad spirits who inhabit the astral. Second, as humans have been in character here on this plane, so will they be when they move out onto the astral plane.

One of the biggest fallacies people have is that people become "good" when they die. Since the emotions go along with the astral body when the physical body dies, a person will be the same as she or he was when alive. If the person in question had strong emotional ties to you (whatever the emotion), and you are still filled with anger, regret, or other intense feelings, then you will sooner or later run into that person on the astral.

Death-bed repentances never take permanently; these promises are made out of fear of what is to come. How many times have you promised yourself you wouldn't do something again, but repeated the action when the next occasion arose? You have to face responsibility and clean up your life before you die in order to reach the astral plane in a positive form.

So while astral journeying, whether you are dealing with discarnate beings or other astral travelers, choose your companions wisely. Laying down with dogs and getting up with fleas applies as much to the astral as it does to Earth. Astral entities, as well as humans, have auras; these auras contain energy particles which can transfer from one aura to another. You want to attract positive energy particles to your aura. Hanging around on the astral with entities that aren't of a high quality may find you with energy particles of a type you don't want. Then you have extra work getting rid of these "fleas."

When speaking of the astral levels, the words "higher" and "lower" have nothing to do with social classes, outward appearance while on Earth, what church you went to, or the amount of time a person spent in worship. Rather, these terms indicate areas of existence inhabited by evolved or devolved souls. A spirit earns its place on a level by her/his past earthly life and true spiritual seeking. This is the real meaning of karma.

Why should you want to astral travel, especially if you don't want to become a peeping tom (which is an unethical occupation)? There are a great many benefits of astral travel, and some unusual but pleasant things to be experienced.

Cornelius Agrippa wrote in *Occult Philosophy* that the human can gain prophetic power by astral travel. The astral traveler is not limited by time, distance, or physical ability. You can go anywhere, any time. There are things which can be accomplished on the astral plane that may be difficult to do or manifest on the physical. And since every manifested thing or event must first come into existence on the astral, you can do healing or magick with a greater proficiency there.

The astral body has fewer limitations in what it can do than the physical body. You learn in meditation that you can instantly be where you want by thinking of that place. Paracelsus, in his *Selected Writings*, wrote that the astral body can go through walls without harm or destruction. This is very true; what would be a physical barrier to the physical body is no barrier at all to the astral body. A person in the physical may be able to see you, if she/he is particularly psychic, but the person can't detain you, take hold of you, or hamper you in any way.

To really begin to understand the astral plane, you must take an open-minded look at what is believed about the astral by various spiritual traditions around the world.

The ancient Egyptians were well aware that humans had more than just a physical body. Although much of the esoteric meaning has been lost, their records state that humankind had seven souls. They called these the *khat* (physical body), *ka* (double), *ab* (heart), *ba* (soul), *khu* or *aakhu* (spirit-soul), *khaibit* (shadow), *sah* or *sahu* (spiritual body), and *sekhem* (willpower or purpose). It is very difficult to know the details of exactly what they meant by all of these terms, but the Egyptians quite clearly believed that the *sah* held the total of all incarnations and returned to the astral planes upon death of the physical body.

These ancient Egyptian descriptions of the souls seem to correspond to the seven light centers and the seven astral levels in some way. Unfortunately, we no longer have any information to help us understand the connection.

The kahunas of Hawaii say there are three spirit bodies, called *kino* (body) *aka* (shadowy). They believed that these three souls are conscious or low self, *unihipili*; subconscious or middle self, *uhane*; and superconscious or high self, *aumakua*. The shadow body of the conscious is the thickest and appears to stay closest to the physical body; this may correspond to the innermost part of the aura, that tiny dark outline next to the body. The shadow body of the subconscious interpenetrates the physical body, being a perfect mold of every cell. The superconscious soul was thought to be the thinnest and finest; this appears as brilliant white light in the aura.

The kahuna description of the subconscious shadow body, the *uhane,* may well be what we call the astral body. It is said to be sticky, meaning that it puts out a tiny thread to everything we touch, see, or think about. This may be the explanation of friends who can send telepathic messages to each other. It might also explain why we find it difficult to break off friendships or relationships. This sticky thread connection may also explain the creation of thoughtforms, for the thread would be a source of electrical energy which the thoughtform could use to become an entity.

The Upanishads of India tell of two invisible bodies, which they call the causal *(karana sharira)* and the subtle *(sukshma sharira).* The third body is, of course, the gross physical. While the Hawaiian kahunas list three strengths of *mana,* or energy, the Hindus give a classification of *prana* (energy) to every known action of the mind and body.

There is no definitive road map for travel on the astral plane and its levels. Each of us discovers our own way there and back. By observation, we learn to take note of markers which will enable us to return to or avoid an area. As with any journey, you decide where you want to go and make preparations as to what you want to take along. Have a definite goal in mind when you travel into the astral, or you may find yourself on a back road that's unpleasant. Be truthful about your motives, and keep a strict watch on negative emotions. Astral travel is a pleasant, fulfilling experience. Embark on your journey with positive expectations, and you won't be disappointed.

Three

Traveling Through Meditation

Meditation is a viable method of astral traveling, although most people don't realize they can use it in this manner. They have read books which say the only way you can astral travel is to will yourself out of your body. When their efforts at this "willing" fail, they either decide they don't have what it takes to project astrally, or the whole thing is a hoax.

Forget all the myths created to frighten you away from meditation and astral travel. You won't get "stuck" out there somewhere; you won't lose your soul; you won't get lost and find yourself unable to return; you won't die. I knew one meditation teacher who controlled her students by telling them if they meditated without her, they would lose their souls. Totally untrue! However, it is an effective fear tactic to ensure a constant group of followers.

The most commonly described method of attempting astral projection is to sit, eyes closed, and visualize yourself standing in front of your seated physical body. This picture of yourself is to be built up entirely, so that it looks like your reflection in a mirror. Then, bit by bit, one is to transfer consciousness into this astral body. The transfer is complete when you can look back and actually see yourself.

However astral projection comes about, it can be a frightening experience to those who suddenly see their body in one place while their consciousness is obviously in another. Hanging about the ceiling staring down at yourself isn't exactly comforting. In reality, this method of projection of the astral body is pretty advanced and probably shouldn't be undertaken until you are comfortable exiting your physical body in less dramatic ways. Besides, I have known many people who astral travel and never once have they seen their own body.

One of the easiest and most pleasant methods of astral travel can be experienced in deep meditation. You prepare yourself as you usually would for a meditation: soft background music, phone shut off, a place where you won't be disturbed. Sit in a comfortable chair, preferably one with arms so you won't fall to the side when you leave astrally. I've never found this to be a problem, but others might. I don't recommend lying down since this is the usual position for sleep.

For protection during any meditation or astral travel, first visualize yourself surrounded with brilliant white light. This will not only give you protection, but also send a signal that you want contact with only positive entities in the astral realms. Follow this white light protection by seeing yourself standing beside a well; throw into the well all the negative thoughts, people, and problems with which you are dealing in life. This further enforces the subconscious desire to be free of anything negative during the meditation. The subconscious understands only symbolism, not words. By visualizing the light and the well, you are sending symbol-language to your subconscious mind.

Sometimes merely dropping problems into the well isn't enough. One friend said that every time she did, they popped right back out. "I decided something more was needed," she told me. "I visualized a lid to cover the well and, for extra measure, a handle on the side to flush them down. It worked."

Now begin relaxing the physical body, beginning at the feet and toes. Tell each foot to relax; imagine yourself undergoing a gentle massage of the muscles. Then move up to the calf of each leg and repeat the process. Repeat this method entirely through the legs, trunk of the body, arms, neck, and all over the head. Spend extra time working on the muscles of the shoulders, neck, and jaw because these areas reflect stress and tension the most.

As you are working up through the body to the head, you will find yourself pulling your consciousness along with you. The parts of your body from which you have pulled your consciousness will begin to feel heavy, while your consciousness feels very light. If this relaxation and pulling away of consciousness is properly done, you will have no sensory input from the lower areas when you reach the head. It will seem as if you are dissociated from the physical body.

At this point, direct your attention to a place you want to visit, usually an Otherworld realm where you can meet teachers and guides. This meeting place may be a beautiful garden, an ancient temple or sanctuary, or a place in nature. Think of a place or scene that makes you feel comfortable and at one with the spiritual realms. Your teachers will either be waiting for you or will appear shortly after you arrive.

Following is a guided meditation to help you get started in both meditation and astral projection. If you feel you don't get immediate results, decide if you are relaxed enough, expecting too much too soon, or have unreasonable expectations in general. Believe and expect that you can astral travel, but at the same time relax and enjoy whatever happens.

The Astral Garden

Begin your meditation by choosing a safe, comfortable place and chair in which to relax. Soft, non-vocal music will help to mask small background noises. Make certain you won't be disturbed by the telephone or someone coming into the room. Close your eyes and visualize yourself surrounded by white light for protection. Begin the relaxation of your body from the feet up to the head. Take as much time for this relaxation as necessary, but don't dwell too long on it. This will create tension in itself.

See yourself standing by an old well with moss-covered stones. Take all the problems, people, and negative situations in your life and drop them into the well. Don't waste any time watching them fall; just walk away as soon as this dumping is finished.

You find yourself walking along a path in a small grove of trees. You can smell the resinous scent of the evergreens, and hear the rustle of the branches as a soft breeze whispers through them. You touch the rough bark, feeling its texture.

As you continue on your way, you pass out of the trees and into a beautiful flower garden. Beds of all kinds of flowers are intertwined with brick pathways. You can see marble benches, fountains, and statues situated among the beds of brilliant blooms. Spend as much time as you like exploring this garden.

Soon you sit on one of the benches, enjoying the smells and sights of this astral garden. As you sit there, watching the flowers and the insects moving busily among them, listening to the singing birds nearby, you hear someone call your name. Coming toward you along one of the paths is a figure. It is one of your teacher-guides.

This being comes and sits beside you on the bench. Don't be surprised if you receive a hug; you can feel astral entities while you are in the astral yourself. You may or may not get a name for this person at this time. Use your astral eyes to determine if this being is a woman or a man, what she/he looks like, and how the person is dressed. At first you may have a little difficulty hearing or understanding what is said to you. This is normal. The more you relax and let the message go from your teacher's mind directly to yours, the easier communication will become.

Listen carefully to everything that is said to you by this teacher. You can sort it out through common sense when you leave meditation. If you are new to meditation, it will be unusual for your teacher to take you anywhere. This is simply a get-acquainted period. However, she/he may mention past life connections between the two of you. This mention of a past life or lives may explain your fascination with certain cultures or time periods.

Finally, the teacher leads you to one of the fountains. There on the rim of the water basin is a cup which she/he fills with water. You take the cup and look at its design carefully. As you drink the water, you notice how cold it is, how pleasant to the taste.

The teacher takes back the cup and touches you on the forehead with one hand. You feel yourself whirling away into a cloud of brilliant white light. You can see the tiny light particles dancing around and through you. You feel renewed and healed, at peace with yourself. As you think of your physical body, you slide back gently into it.

Slowly open your eyes and stretch. Allow yourself time to readjust to the physical plane. If you stand up too suddenly, you may feel dizzy, disoriented, and may get a headache.

Now is the time to truthfully analyze your astral-meditation. Were you totally unaware of your physical body and its surroundings? Could you see, smell, taste, and feel while you were in the garden? Were the colors extra vivid? Was your teacher real to you? Could you communicate with her/him? When your teacher mentioned a past life, did you feel a sense of rightness?

If you can answer in the positive to half or more of these questions, you were fully astral traveling. If you had some difficulty, don't despair. Keep meditating with gentle expectation. Going into meditation with the tenseness of demanding that you accomplish a particular thing will almost certainly keep you from experiencing it. The trick is to meditate with relaxed expectations. Go to the astral garden to enjoy whatever you see or find. In this way, your progress will be pleasant and much faster than you expect.

Don't judge your success by the amount of time you stay in meditation and/or astral travel. Gradually build up to as much as thirty minutes, but don't set this as an absolutely necessary goal to prove anything. When you wish to return to your physical body, simply think of returning and you will.

I discovered a side benefit for this pulling of consciousness up through the body quite by accident. I used to suffer from migraine headaches brought on by extreme stress in relationships, both personal and professional. One can't hold down a job effectively when drugged out of your skull or with a pounding headache that makes you think you would feel better if you were dead three days. In an effort to escape the excruciating pain, I found that if I pulled my consciousness up through my body and then placed it above my head, all the while repeating "No pain," I could escape. If I stayed in that suspended state for several minutes and came back to reality slowly, I could hold that pain-free state of being. Of course reality was a little strange, but it was better than the pain.

A light finally came on. I realized I was deliberately withdrawing my astral body to escape the pain. When I decided to come back to reality, I was not completely seating the astral body in its usual position; it was connected with the physical body just enough for the body and brain to function properly but not feel any pain. When the migraine went away, the astral body would once more seat itself in its usual position in conjunction with the physical and the world around me would become "real" again.

Meditation can be a satisfying experience even if you don't go deeply. But a true spiritual seeker isn't interested in losing her/himself in a temporary state every time with no objective in mind. A seeker is interested in leaving behind the hindering physical body and conscious mind for a time, while the astral body and the subconscious and superconscious minds search for information and enlightenment.

To reach this deeper stage of meditation, one must practice and be patient. There are no magick words that will propel you into this state of being; only discipline and persistent meditation will enable you to reach it. Relaxation is the biggest key to all astral travel, and reaching astral projection through deep meditation is no exception. You must determine with every fiber of your being that you want to astral travel, but at the same time not allow the tension of this wanting to exist. If you believe you can journey in the astral realms, look forward to the experience, and expect to have a wonderful time, the tension is released automatically.

Upon reaching this relaxed state of separation of the astral from the physical in meditation, you may find yourself looking at your physical body. However, you probably won't. So don't set your criteria of success as seeing yourself in one place while your consciousness is in another. If you are properly relaxed and have achieved astral projection, your physical body will have little meaning to you. In fact, when you are in the astral, none of your usual physical senses will convey any messages to you at all, unless your body is in danger.

Always keep a destination in mind while you are going into meditation. Perhaps you want to meet and talk with your teachers and guides. These beings are sometimes called guardian angels, particularly by those who are uncomfortable with the term guides. You can direct your astral body to a garden, temple, or ancient school where you will be met by your spiritual companions. The choice of destination is yours.

It is a good idea to keep a journal of your Otherworld experiences. This helps you to see patterns, understand spiritual messages, and most of all, determine whether you are hearing just what you want to hear or whether you are allowing the truth to come through.

You will find that in deep meditation, as in astral traveling, colors are more vivid and your senses (which are now separated from the physical) are heightened. You also will find that all your senses work: sight, touch, taste, hearing, smell, emotions. Your thinking processes will be clear and sharp. You may not be familiar with some of the entities and places you see, but don't discount them. You are becoming aware of other planes of existence, perhaps for the first time.

Thoughts between you and any entities you meet are transmitted telepathically rather than verbally. Unlike visiting a foreign country, there is no language barrier. All communications will be in the language you understand best. That doesn't mean you will grasp a complicated spiritual discussion right away. You may need to think about such a discussion, perhaps for months, after you return before you begin to grasp the details that were given to you.

Many people have a bad habit of accepting everything told to them on the astral as something they should implement immediately or must accept without question. Use common sense! Spiritual entities don't look at things as we do. I know people who have gotten divorces, left jobs, or moved to another town on spirit advice without thinking it through. Most of the time they ended up in a worse situation than they were in before. The divorce, job change, or move may have been a beneficial idea, but they hadn't dealt with the problems and responsibilities of the old condition first. It may not have been the perfect time to implement the change. So the problems just moved along with them.

Some people get some very strange, unethical advice during meditation and/or astral travel. You can bet these people aren't being truthful with themselves about their desires and actions in life. They were hearing just what they wanted to hear and have drawn low-level guides to themselves.

Martha was in a marriage she considered "bad." Neither she nor her husband would consider a divorce, although there had been no physical relationship for about five years. They barely spoke to each other. In fact, she made no bones that she prayed for him to die. During meditation, Martha was told that her husband would die within a year and she would get everything she wanted: the house, his pension, etc. She refused to look truthfully at the situation and her own attitude, but continued telling everyone that she would soon be free. Six years later the husband finally did die, but Martha ended up without the house or the pension.

When we are involved with something unethical, for instance, we will draw to us only unethical guides. Your teachers and guides will be equal only to your true desire for spiritual growth and knowledge. If you want to draw higher spiritual teachers, you need to clean up your act, accept responsibility for your actions and life, and look at your life without blinders. Preconceived thought, strongly held, will override the truth in meditation every time.

Travel from one place to another in Otherworld or astral realms is extremely easy. At first you may find yourself thinking you have to walk or fly from place to place, propelling yourself by motions of your arms and legs. This is a common assumption since physically that is how you have to move about. However, you can move instantly to wherever you want to go by thinking yourself there. You may choose to "physically" stroll through a beautiful place simply to enjoy the surroundings. I do this with a particular rose garden I visit. To move any distance, you can think yourself there and be there in an instant, as quick as the thought itself. A good comparison is light, which travels at the speed of 186,000 miles per second.

Some time or another you will probably have a "bad trip." Discounting what will be seen under the use of drugs or alcohol, such experiences usually happen because of emotional problems. If anyone thinks the intellect rules the emotions, just go into meditation while under emotional strain. You will change your thoughts about the intellect's power.

Although you think you have emotional tensions under control, you will find they transform into weird and sometimes scary images in the astral. At one time when I was trying to cope with intense emotional problems in connection with two unethical people, I would often find myself struggling through a frightening jungle of trees and vines. It was such a suffocating feeling that the only course was to end the meditation. I couldn't will myself into any other surroundings. As soon as I dealt with the problem and released the emotional ties, I was once again able to place myself in the usual comforting, beautiful scenery.

Negative and/or emotional upheavals can also draw to you astral entities who are not of a high spiritual quality. Alcoholics and drug users often tell of seeing threatening or demon-like entities; they are attracting entities who match their own ethical and spiritual levels. These people have reached the very lowest levels of the astral plane where this type of entity dwells. If this happens to you, and you are not involved with mind-altering substances, take a good, truthful look at yourself. Are you involved in unethical behavior? Are you allowing intense negative emotions to consume your thoughts? If you want to get to the higher astral levels, you had better make some positive changes in your life and thinking.

Reflection upon these types of astral experiences will show you that your emotions merely ignored the directions of your intellect. The emotion, one you thought was well out of the way, causing your astral distress may be buried in your subconscious mind. You have to drag it out into the conscious mind, acknowledge its existence, and deal with it in a positive way. You never eliminate negative emotions by simply stifling and trying to bury them.

If you are full of anger and resentment when you meditate or go out on the astral, you are deliberately courting a negative experience. If you are caught up in the wild desires of lust or craving for something (a physical person or an object), your astral body will carry these emotions along with it, taking you to a corresponding spiritual level, which I assure you won't be where you want to go. Because the astral body does carry emotions with it, some traditions call it the desire or emotional body.

An example of this was a woman who suspected her husband was cheating on her. She was full of fear and anger. She had many clues, tangible and subconscious, which led her to believe this was so. But every time she attempted to astral travel to check on him, she ended up with some very upsetting astral destinations, not even getting close to her husband and his girlfriend. Finally, she gave up and made her decisions to leave, based on her unhappy life and the treatment she received from her husband. On her next astral-meditation she once more found her spiritual teacher who praised her for taking responsibility. Then, as a side-benefit, this teacher gave her a clear view of the husband with several girlfriends, calling each woman by name. The wife noted the information but felt no further animosity; she had already severed the ties. When the husband vowed he would fight the divorce, she simply rattled off the women's names. His aggressive attitude deflated like a punctured balloon. She went on to build a productive, happy life, while the ex-husband is still wallowing in self-pity.

When you go out onto the astral plane, whether it be by meditation, dreaming, or any other method, you take with you all the emotions, positive or negative, that are clinging to your life. You are responsible for where you go on the astral and what you see by truthfully acknowledging and dealing with your emotional problems. This often takes a lot of painful self-discipline, but the benefits are worth it. Living in a state of denial simply denies you spiritual growth. The choice is yours.

What does all this have to do with astral travel? A lot!

There is a wide variety of variations and degrees of astral travel and experiences. You can't really believe in astral projection and travel until you experience it for yourself. And you can't experience it (at least in a positive way) unless you keep an open mind, change your life into a positive mode, and are prepared to believe your experiences while using common sense.

How do you know if you are astral traveling during meditation? If you are totally unaware of your physical body while meditating, you are out on the astral. If your meditative visits are vivid and you are actively participating in the action, you are astral traveling. If you have had meaningful conversations and received prophetic information (that came true) from astral entities, you were truly on the astral levels—and you haven't once had to look back at your old confining, limited, physical body to prove you were doing it right.

Ceremonial magicians and Qabalists have been going onto the astral plane for centuries by using a method similar to meditation. They concentrate on the Tree of Life glyph, working their way up through the central pillar from the Earth sphere (sephiroth) to the spiritual spheres. By visualizing their way along this central pillar, they project themselves deliberately onto high spiritual planes. By studying the characteristics of each sphere through which they must pass, they understand all the emotional baggage that can be attached to their astral bodies. Thus, when they don't get where they want to go, they look for a particular emotion associated with the sphere on which they were stuck.

You can do the same thing, without becoming a ceremonial magician or studying the complicated Qabala. By relating your astral images to your emotional state or the emotional difficulties in your life, you can determine what you need to change in order to reach a higher level.

It is also possible to meet other astral travelers while you are "out and about," as the Scots say. Most of them you will never meet in their physical forms. Some of these travelers will be beginners, struggling to learn all they can, just like you. Others will be experienced astral wanderers, seeking more advanced knowledge. A very few will have reached almost the "master" status. Some of these people will have deliberately traveled onto the astral, while others will be there during sleep or while undergoing a state of physical crisis, like an accident or surgery.

It is quite common to meet shamans, magicians, witches and other Pagans, spiritual seekers of all kinds from all cultures journeying through the astral planes. Most of them have goals similar to yours: spiritual enlightenment and the seeking of information. You can communicate with them, if they are willing. Some of these people, who are physically separated by great distances, hold group gatherings on the astral at regular intervals. Always ask permission before you barge into such a meeting.

You need to judge the character of spiritual entities and/or astral travelers in the same way as you do when you meet people in their physical bodies. Use common sense! When you meet such a traveler (or any astral entity), be aware of how you feel about her or him. Your intuitive senses are highly sharpened in the astral and can be trained to be quite reliable. If the actions, words, or the feelings emanating from these astral travelers or spirits make you uncomfortable or afraid, move yourself to another area. If necessary, end the astral travel. After all, you have every right to choose who you want around you.

At some time it is inevitable that you will meet an astral traveler or entity who makes you feel afraid or uncomfortable. When you come back to your body, analyze your emotions to see if you attracted such a traveler or entity through your own personal problems. Be truthful. If you lie to yourself, the person you hurt will be you! If you didn't attract her/him/it through some fault of your own, analyze what this being's presence may mean to you. If you would have been attracted to this type of person in the past, your teachers may have been testing you to see if your spiritual and emotional changes were firm.

The good astral experiences, however, will far outweigh those you consider "bad." By truthfully persevering in your search for development of your spiritual soul, you can evolve much faster if you use a combination of physical and astral study. This is the most important reason for learning to astral travel. A large amount of knowledge given to you while astral traveling will not be available on this plane of existence. That information has been lost or destroyed.

When you get tired of wandering around on the astral planes, you can find teachers who will impart wonderful and helpful knowledge. Wandering about is a common occupation for beginning astral travelers. When a child first learns to walk, she/he just wants to go everywhere with no productive destination in mind. Later, the child learns to set goals, such as "walking across the kitchen will help me reach Momma, who will give me a cookie." So, beginning astral travelers learn to set the "cookie" goal. They find a teacher who will instruct them in the knowledge they seek. It's only later that the astral traveler learns to change the goal from "getting the cookies" to "making the cookies." This is hands-on work, such as healing and magick, often under the supervision of a teacher.

Some of these teachers work with beginners, while others teach more advanced classes. If you manage to get into a group learning advanced material, you may find that you can't understand a single word of what is being said. This is a clue that you are in over your head. A polite request for help will bring you a teacher more on your present level.

The first time this happened to me, I wasn't sure what was going on. I was drawn to the spiritual teacher because he gave off such a brilliant glow. But he, and everyone grouped around him, seemed to be speaking in some foreign language. No matter how I strained to understand, nothing made any sense. Finally, the teacher smiled at me and said clearly, "You're in the wrong class." One of the young men got up and escorted me to a Greek temple where the priestess laughed and said, "You always want the details before you understand the basics." She

33

certainly knew me well; I'm an impatient person when I decide to do or learn something.

Some astral teachers specialize in certain knowledge. A great many of these instructors are from ancient civilizations and times, some of whose history is now lost to us. Even the ancient records we do know about are incomplete and/or the esoteric underlying mystical knowledge long forgotten. There are teachers who can instruct you in art, music, history, ancient ceremonies, mystic secrets—any subject you can imagine.

There are also special counselors who work with the Akashic records, the repository of information about every single past life of a particular person. They can help you look at your past lives, analyze what now affects you, and how you can make changes to avoid further painful experiences. Karma is both positive and negative; it is put into action by both the good and bad actions and decisions you made in the past. Don't fall for the lie that karma is involved with every negative thing that happens to you. It isn't that simple.

The novice at first looks into her/his Akashic records for thrills. Was I important and powerful? Was I famous? This is a normal reaction, but be aware that it's very unlikely you were some famous historical figure. After all, the world is run primarily by the actions and reactions of the everyday person in the street, not by some member of royalty or head of government who doesn't know how to cook a meal.

Searching through your Akashic records soon takes on another perspective. You begin to see relationship patterns, behavior traits, buried talents, even physical problems. The thread of these traits, relationships, problems, and talents may run through several lives, right down to and including the present one.

If you are sincere, your Akashic counselor will reveal to you the connections between present and past relationships. This can be a great eye-opener, especially if you are presently uncertain about continuing or ending a friendship or relationship. Just because you loved or lived with someone in another life does not make this individual your ideal mate or friend this time. You need to look for buried emotions in those lives that you might have missed at the time: jealousy, a need to control, intimidation, revenge, possessiveness. If you find such a thread, don't accept that it occurred only in one lifetime. Follow it back as close to the beginning of the problem as you can get. You may or may not have initiated the trouble, but you needn't continue it.

There is an ancient saying about karma that is little known: "Never teach karma to anyone not willing and prepared to overcome it." The only reason to look through your Akashic records is to make yourself a better person. The responsibility falls right back on you: your reactions, your attitudes, your desires, your morals, your spiritual goals. Understanding these threads of consequence from the past may give you clues to present illnesses and/or difficulties, personal or otherwise.

Charles suffered from severe headaches as far back as he could remember. Nothing seemed to keep them away very long. While exploring through his Akashic records, he came upon a lifetime as a fur trapper who lived with his wife in the mountains. His horse fell, and Charles received a head wound that troubled him the rest of that life. The pain was persistent enough that it became ingrained. By understanding where the pain originated, he was able to reject it as unnecessary this time.

However, the Akashic records are not only repositories of past problems. You may discover long-forgotten talents that you can relearn today. Some of these talents may be beyond your present scope of relearning, but others will not be. If you decide you want to delve into these talents, learn all you can in the physical, but also astral travel to skilled teachers who can help you. To receive this guidance, you have to regularly astral travel, become familiar with your astral surroundings, and set high spiritual goals. Skilled teachers don't reside on the lower levels. Like any teacher, they expect you to keep a regular schedule of classes.

Looking Through Your Akashic Records

Begin your meditation with the usual physical preparation as well as with the white light, relaxation, and problem-dumping.

Return to the astral garden and wait for your teacher-guide. Soon after you arrive, this teacher will appear. Follow her/him through the garden to a temple. The temple can be any form from a pyramid to an ancient temple.

The two of you go inside, where it is dimly lit and pleasant. She/he leads the way to a huge room filled with scrolls and what appear to be long shelves of books. There is a long table with a top of inlaid crystal in the center of the room; comfortable chairs are set around this table.

Your teacher motions for you to sit at the table. She/he wanders off through the shelves of books and soon returns with a huge volume. As the book is laid on the table before you, look closely at the cover and the binding. Is there writing on it you can read? If you can't, ask your teacher to interpret for you.

Open the book and turn through the pages. There will be writing and pictures throughout the book. Your teacher will help you if you find you can't read the language. Inside the back cover in a little pocket is a crystal square. Take it out and place it on the crystal tabletop in front of you.

Scenes from the book will appear in motion, sound, and full color on the tabletop, rather like watching a movie. Does the life or culture depicted in the crystal seem familiar to you? Ask all the questions you want of your teacher. You may be told that some things will be explained in full at a later time. Take this politely, for you probably aren't ready to see or understand something yet.

If you have specific questions pertaining to an immediate problem in your life, ask your teacher-guide at this time. Listen closely to the answer; let yourself be sensitive to the feelings directed to you by this teacher.

The teacher places the crystal square back into the book and returns the book to its place on the shelf. Now you can go back into the garden or ask to be directed to a place for a meditation within a meditation.

Whenever you are ready to return to your physical body, simply call the white light to surround you. Think of your body and feel yourself slide gently back into it.

Once you have the "feel" of the building which houses the Akashic records, you can return to it at any time. There is always an astral being there to help with research until you learn how to find the books you want by yourself.

The meditation within a meditation is quite an experience if properly done. It is not unusual to find yourself projected into another area or level of the astral plane, or even being summoned before a deity. This is a very special spiritual experience that can leave you on a "high" for some time afterward.

At some point in your research through the many volumes of your Akashic records, you will discover it is possible to look into the records of other people. Don't be a snoop! It's no more ethical to randomly look through someone's past than it is to peek through her/his bedroom window.

It is perfectly ethical to look into the records of people who have a direct bearing on your life, such as business associates, close friends, lovers, or people trying to become close to you in any way. It is also ethical, and perhaps vital, that you look into the Akashic records of anyone not close to you but creating problems, such as stalkers, troublesome neighbors, or similar people. You may discover a past unresolved problem between these people and you, or you may simply find that the person has a long history of negative behavior.

I have found, as have many psychics, that a great many of the young men of today who are drawn to gangs and/or violent behavior have past lives as soldiers in more than one culture. Most have a history of continuing lifetimes in this occupation. They are involved in their present activity because they like what they are doing; they enjoy frightening others and hurting or killing them. Therefore, they have chosen to be born into a situation that enables them to continue experiencing these thrills.

Max had a childhood no worse than most people, but he always demanded that he should have more, be treated with great deference, and never be responsible for his actions. Even at a very young age he looked down upon women. His mother Leta did everything she could, but it was never enough. By fifth grade, Max was in constant trouble with teachers, the authorities, and other parents. His chosen companions were always those whom he could control or who looked up to him as leader. He always expected to be bailed out whenever he got into trouble and never be blamed or receive punishment. He stole money and jewelry from his mother and others. When Max finally turned eighteen, Leta kicked him out of the house—a difficult and dangerous task, since Max was prone to physical violence.

Leta and I decided to look into Max's Akashic records separately, then compare notes. We discovered the same details. Max had once been a spoiled, rich young Frenchman during the 1700s. Because of his family's status and money, he did what he pleased without consequences. He was cruel, a bully, and ended his life in a midnight duel with a better swordsman. The fight had been over Leta, who even in that lifetime hadn't found him to be a pleasant person, but had felt sorry for him.

Understanding the past life connections, Leta decided that even if Max was her son this time didn't mean she had to put up with his unacceptable behavior. She had struggled to progress spiritually, while Max had chosen to remain as he had been. Leta established new rules for her life; she is polite but distant with Max and his continuing problems.

The more you make meditation a regular part of your life, the easier it is to astral travel. The vividness of these travels during meditation will intensify; your senses will experience even more, and to a new height, than you do while in the physical. Stresses in everyday life will diminish. You will find yourself making better choices in everything from choosing a friend or lover to setting goals. You will also find that astral travel sharpens whatever psychic abilities you have, and may well open up new ones. There is so much to be gained by meditation coupled with astral travel that one should make such activity a frequent and established part of one's life.

Four

Sleep and Astral Projection

Everyone astral travels whenever they sleep; most people just don't realize what they are doing or haven't trained themselves to remember it. If your "dreams" include flying or gliding, vivid colors, active participation in the action, or conversations with entities who tell you things that later come true, you are astral traveling during your sleep. It is a normal human function that has been occurring since the human race came into existence.

The astral energy which makes up this body by which we travel, leaving the physical behind, can actually be photographed during special circumstances. This is called Kirlian photography. In the early 1940s, a Russian scientist, Semyon Kirlian, began studying what he called bioplasma and discovered how it could be photographed. Mystics around the world know this bio-plasma as the aura. It exists around every physical object, with living organisms having a much brighter and bigger field of energy.

Later, in France, scientists began to wonder if they could measure the "soul" at death. They began to weigh dying people and discovered a discrepancy of a few ounces which they could not explain. Dr. Duncan McDougall in England and Dr. Zaalberg Van Zelst in The Hague, working independently, came to the same conclusion. These doctors both arrived at the same dis-placed amount: 69.5 grams. Then they took some very startling photos with infrared rays. These pictures showed a luminous cloud, the exact outline of the body, exiting at the time of death. This luminous form is the astral body, what is seen by psychics and sensitive people when you astral travel to them.

Although you can astral travel during sleep without any preparation, you can be more productive if you plan for it. Preparing for astral travel during sleep is much the same as preparing for meditation in many aspects. Visualize yourself sur-rounded by white light; breathe it in by taking several deep, slow breaths. See yourself discarding all problems into a well. Begin relaxing the body from the feet up to the head. Pull your con-sciousness up along with the relaxation until you feel yourself above your physical head. Then allow yourself to drift into sleep.

I experienced one very interesting side-effect of this prepa-ration and didn't know for a long time that anyone else had seen the same thing. As I lay relaxed and ready for sleep, I could see the room bathed in a greenish glow. The first time this happened I naturally opened my eyes. I assumed that my eyes had been open all the time. Being too much of an analytical person at times, I had failed to realize that I wasn't using my physical eyes to see the room, but my astral eyes. By staying relaxed and clos-ing my eyes again, I could once more see every object and the room itself filled with this green mist. What I was seeing was the astral mist which often precedes astral travel.

As in meditation, you should have a goal in mind if you deliberately plan to astral travel during sleep. If you don't know where you want to go, at least call upon your guides to direct your nightly wanderings. You don't want to be journeying unexpectedly in some unpleasant section of astral territory. And be sure to record what you consider to be your nightly astral travels. By recording your experiences, your subconscious mind will reveal to you the meaning of symbols, connect threads of travel that repeat through several journeys, sort out past life "movies," and bring to your attention which "dreams" are actually prophecies.

When you are out on the astral, you may or may not see the silver cord which connects your astral body with your physical body. There are a variety of opinions on where this cord is connected. I've known some people to see it attached to their ankle, while others see it coming from their solar plexus. If I'm aware of the silver cord at all, I see it attached to the center of my forehead, evidently connected in some way to the brow chakra. I don't think there is one universal location to where the silver cord is attached; it's enough to know it exists and is your connection at all times with the physical body.

Those people who actively want to discourage exploration into the astral come up with all kinds of horror stories about the silver cord being severed by evil entities. The negative beings I've met on rare occasions haven't been interested in my silver cord, but in me. If you surround yourself with white light before going to sleep, you won't be in any danger from such unscrupulous entities, even though you may feel uncomfortable. They most certainly can't sever your connecting cord and possess your body, leaving you stranded in some limbo.

Sometimes during nightly astral travel, you may find yourself reliving a part of another lifetime. In these cases, you probably have projected yourself into the Akashic records temple and are viewing one of your books. If some event in a past life made an intense emotional impact on you, you may continue to "dream" about it until you face it squarely and know it for what it is: something that happened long ago. Such a "dream" may occur because a similar situation is threatening to occur in your present life, or a person connected with that past life has once more moved close to you.

As far back as I could recall dreams, I experienced a recurring nightmare. I would find myself running down a dirt road in the dark. My heart would be pounding in terror. I knew I had to get down the road, over the steep bank, and into the trees and bushes. If I didn't, whoever was after me would kill me. The dream never had any other scenes but this one. It repeated itself for years until I stumbled upon the answer when I learned to meditate.

As I sat in the Akashic records temple viewing a past life in France, I saw the whole "nightmare" replayed, this time with an ending. I was a very young woman and had committed a breach of ethics of the day—I had fallen in love with a German soldier. A war between France and Germany was in progress and I was caught with hundreds of other country people in the middle of the fighting. As we struggled down that dirt road at night, over the bank, and through the trees, we came to a cave where we hid. It wasn't long before the German soldiers tracked us down and began killing us.

As I turned to flee, there was a sharp pain in my lower back. I could actually feel the blood under my hands on the cave floor as I tried to pull myself away. The last scene was when I reached out and touched the toe of a soldier's boot. When I looked up, I saw the sadistic, smiling face of my lover, a man with whom I had a present relationship.

The shock was so great that I exited that meditation immediately. There was absolutely no doubt in my mind that what I saw had happened. I immediately began a series of plans to rid myself of that person in this life. Although up to that time the man in question had displayed no violent tendencies, he showed his true character at once. It took some very determined effort to get him out of my life permanently.

Later I discovered that this control-possession-cruelty relationship had begun in yet another life, further back in time, when in a Viking raid he didn't get me as his share of the spoils. He had developed a fixation to have and to hurt me at that time. Strong emotions, positive or negative, can be carried through several lifetimes. Recognizing what the "nightmare" signified and taking action on what I learned released me. I never had that dream again.

Herbs, Stones, and Oils

Oftentimes, we need a little help in recalling astral travel and/or heightening the psychic senses we all have, some more than others. You don't want to turn to harmful drugs. One of the easiest, and most pleasant, ways to do this is through the use of herbs, stones, and oils.

To heighten the psychic senses during astral travel, you can use a dream pillow. This is simple to make and non-toxic. Cut out two squares of cloth about eight inches long by six inches wide. Place the two right sides of the cloth together and stitch a narrow seam around three of the edges. Turn this bag so that the seams are now on the inside. Stuff this little pillow with dried mugwort, an herb long known for its ability to enhance the psychic. Stitch the opening closed.

To use this dream pillow, place it under your regular pillow when you go to bed at night. Use your normal procedure of preparation for nightly astral travel by surrounding yourself with the white light, relaxing the body, and pulling your consciousness up above your head. Then go to sleep as usual.

When Leslie heard of my dream pillow, she wanted one. She always declared herself open to psychic messages, so I felt comfortable in giving her one. Within a week Leslie informed me she no longer used the pillow as her dreams became strange and unsettling. I suggested that she might be looking through her Akashic records at other lifetimes. Her mouth set in a firm line, and she told me that wasn't so. I knew she was seeing another man although she was married, so I deduced the "dreams" had something to do with the situation.

Soon afterward Leslie miscarried; the baby was not her husband's. The marriage exploded, with vicious recriminations on both sides. One of her close friends later mentioned that Leslie had seen bits of this future in the "dreams" and rejected the information because she was set on going ahead with what she was doing.

If you don't want to face the truth, don't sleep with a dream pillow. You will be presented with information, sometimes in a realistic sense, other times symbolic, that will have a direct bear-

43

ing on your present life. No one, physical or spiritual, will force you to take positive action on this information. The responsibility for your life and actions is yours alone. However, if you continually reject all such information as untrue, you will likely find that you have cut off your pipeline to the psychic. You will still astral travel; that's a normal sleep process. But you will be unlikely to remember much, if any, of it.

Using certain stones to help with astral travel during sleep is another safe method of enhancing and intensifying your experiences. These stones can be polished and set into jewelry, tumbled smooth, or left in their natural state. I personally don't like sleeping in jewelry other than rings, so I use the stones unset.

Stones can be selected according to their ancient uses. You can use more than one stone at a time, if you wish. If you choose an unset stone, place it under your pillow at night. If your astral excursions are too intense and make you uncomfortable, try placing the stone on the nightstand near the bed instead.

Also be aware that your physical body and aura change from time to time in their patterns of electrical energy pulses. This may cause you to be comfortable with a stone one time, but uncomfortable with the same stone too close to you a few months later. Use common sense and adjust the stone usage until you find a comfortable compromise. In a few months your pattern of energy pulses will very likely readjust itself, and you can again use the stone at a close range.

Amethyst: The amethyst has been considered a high vibrational spiritual stone for centuries. Some writers state that this stone is associated with the pineal gland, which would connect it with the brow center, although its violet color seems to join it with the crown center. It is said to be good to ease insomnia, hate, fear, great anger, grief, and hallucinations. Magickally, it is excellent for spiritual journeying, which makes amethyst a valuable astral travel gem.

Aquamarine: The clear blue or blue-green color of this gem reminds one of the sea; its name means "sea-water." It is a stone prized by seers and mystics, since the ancients considered aquamarine to reinforce psychic impressions and give a clarity to mental visions. For astral travel, this stone aids in common sense and a clear mind.

Azurite: Although ancient cultures did not mention azurite by this name, it is quite possible that they knew it under another title; this was very common and makes it difficult sometimes for us to determine what they mean when they use a name that is unknown to us today. When azurite is cut in a cabochon shape, its reflecting surface looks much like a peacock feather. Azurite aids with psychic development.

Crystal, Quartz: This stone, sometimes known as rock crystal, is well known to almost every culture. The specimens found in Ireland were called God stones and were often buried with the dead, a custom also known to Native Americans. Crystals were sold by European apothecaries as late as 1750 for healing purposes. Quartz crystal can help open the psychic centers.

Lapis lazuli: This stone was known to the ancient Egyptians as the "Stone of Heaven." They made jewelry and scarab images out of it. Its spiritual significance was acknowledged as far away as old Mexico. Lapis lazuli is said to promote deep, sound sleep with its high spiritual vibrations. In astral travel, this stone will aid in spiritual vision.

Malachite: This ancient stone is making a slow comeback in popularity today. It is a dark green stone, often marked with lighter green concentric circles which appear when properly cut. Malachite gives a feeling of general well-being, and positive and prosperous thought.

Moonstone: To me, the moonstone is the most fascinating stone there is. When properly cut, an eye-like shimmer will move across its surface. Tradition says it changes with the phases of the Moon, waxing and waning as the Moon does. In India, the moonstone is called the dreamstone. It helps to unmask enemies.

Peridot: This is a light green stone that is little known. It must have been called by another name in ancient times, for we do not find it listed as such in old records. It promotes sleep.

Tourmaline, Blue: This stone comes in more than one color: red, pink, green, yellow-green, honey-yellow, black, violet, and blue. Sometimes there is more than one color in a single stone. Blue tourmaline will calm nervousness and give confidence and inspiration.

Essential oils have been used for as long as humans have known about them. Every essential oil known to us today has a history of ancient magickal uses behind it. Before using any such oil on your body, place a tiny amount on the inside of your elbow to check for allergy and sensitivity. Some oils are highly toxic and irritating, so read fully about them before using them directly on your body or in bath water. The safest method of use would be to put a drop or two on a cotton ball, then place the cotton on the nightstand next to your bed.

It is an ancient tradition in many cultures that the scent of specific essential oils reacts on the psychic senses and light centers of the astral body. Smelling crushed herbs or fresh flowers can be substituted for some of the oils. *Never* ingest any essential oil! Some of them are very harmful if used in this way.

Use only one oil (herb or flower) at a time, or you may get a jumble of astral experiences. You want your recollections of these travels to be clear, not confused.

Bay: Wreath-crowns of bay laurel leaves were given to victors by the ancient Greeks. Bay was sacred to Apollo, Sun god and later ruler of the Delphic oracle. It promotes psychic awareness.

Calendula: The common name for this flower is marigold. I personally don't care for the odor of the fresh flowers; they tend to give me a headache, as do tulips. The name comes from the Latin *calends*, which was their first day of every month. It is said to produce psychic dreams.

Chamomile: I love the apple odor of fresh Roman chamomile. Its name came from the Greek *chamaimelon* ("Earth apple"). However, German (or vulgar) chamomile has an acrid, bitter smell.

Chamomile tea has been used for centuries as a sedative at bed-time. It produces restful sleep and relieves tensions.

Cinnamon: To most people, the smell of cinnamon brings back pleasant memories of their mothers' baking, usually during the Winter Solstice season. The oil causes extreme irritation, so don't use it on your skin. It can produce psychic awareness.

Clary sage: Although related to common garden sage, clary sage is different in scent and growth. It also is not toxic in oil form, as common sage can be. Some people don't care for the odor of this herb at all. Its musty scent is said to promote calmness and dreams.

Deer's tongue: This herb smells much like vanilla. It is used by many readers of the tarot, runes, etc. to enhance their psychic awareness. It will do the same at night for astral travel.

Frankincense: Don't use this oil on your skin; it will cause irritation. The use of this oil goes back at least 3000 years. It makes one more aware of spiritual realms, reduces stress, and releases the conscious mind's control over the superconscious mind.

Honeysuckle: In magick, honeysuckle is often connected with increasing money. This sweet flower also has another attribute—the increasing of psychic awareness.

Hyacinth: The overpowering, sweet odor of this flower gives me a headache. However, ancient tradition states that it is effective in stopping nightmares and promoting a peaceful sleep.

Iris: The dried root of the Florentine iris is called orris root. Its scent reminds me of dusty dried violets. The odor of this flower root or oil is said to strengthen the connection between the conscious mind and the psychic centers.

Jasmine: Pure jasmine oil is extremely expensive. The odor of the oil or flowers reacts directly on the emotional centers. It quiets nervousness and promotes spirituality and psychic dreams.

Lilac: Nowadays the scent of lilac is said to drive away ghosts. Originally, however, its scent was used in ancient mystery schools to promote far-memory, or recalling past lives.

Lotus or water lily: The lotus was widely known and used throughout the ancient Middle East, India, and Egypt. Inhaling this scent gives peace and tranquility.

Mace: Mace is connected with nutmeg, as it comes from the membrane covering the nuts. It is a very strong, spicy odor that enhances psychic awareness.

Mimosa: The yellow flowers of the mimosa have a sweet smell. Unlike the lilac, connected with far-memory, the mimosa encourages psychic dreams of the future. It is also said to aid in understanding dream symbols.

Mugwort: This oil is hazardous! Use the plant instead. For centuries, mugwort has been used by seers and mystics as an aid in divination. The leaves are rubbed on crystal balls to strengthen their power. Its odor also promotes psychic dreams and astral travel itself.

Myrrh: The use of myrrh goes back as far as the use of frankincense, if not farther. Its scent is bitter, which is why it is often mixed with frankincense. The scent of myrrh aids in meditation and enhancing one's awareness of the spiritual realms.

Nutmeg: Toxic in large quantities, so don't use on the skin or in the bath water! Nutmeg is ordinarily associated with memories of eggnog and baking. However, it has been used for a long time as an opener of the psychic centers.

Sandalwood: This word comes from the Sanskrit *chandana*. It is primarily imported from India, but the tree is also found on several Pacific islands. It helps with meditation and raising one's spiritual vibrations.

Star anise: The star anise, the dried fruit of an Eastern tree, looks like an eight-point star and smells like licorice. Its odor promotes psychic awareness.

Yarrow: This garden flower has a rich scent. Its odor helps calm the conscious mind to the point where it allows psychic communication to take place.

There are many other appropriate oils, herbs, and stones which can be used to enhance astral projection, travel, and adventures. Any of the books by Scott Cunningham (published by Llewellyn Publications) are excellent for this information.

Astral travel remembered during sleep can often give you a feeling of being on a journey where you have no control over the itinerary. You need to develop faith in your teacher-guides to present you with the needed and necessary information to help you in your life. The closer your relationship with them, the more explicit your astral travels will be.

If you have asked to study during your nightly astral travels, you may find that, after a few weeks of this, you wake up as tired as when you went to bed. Sometimes it begins to feel as if you are cramming for college exams. In cases such as this, you need to have a straight-forward talk with your teachers and tell them to let up on the pressure a little. Do this politely, of course, as they can literally take you at your word.

I went through a couple of months of this nightly teaching, so intense that I dragged through the day. Finally, I rebelled and yelled out loud, "Knock it off, guys. I need my rest." I suddenly found myself deprived of that astral schooling entirely. In order to resume the classes, I found it necessary to go into meditation, apologize, and ask for a lighter "school" load.

Since everyone astral travels during sleep, whatever they feel about the subject of the astral, those who are seeking spiritual enlightenment and aid from the astral planes for their everyday life should attempt to make productive use of the journeys.

To do this, first you must accept the fact that you do astral travel. Then you need to ask for spiritual help in remembering the travels and/or "dreams." If you have established a close relationship with your teacher-guides through meditation, this will be much easier.

In order to have a productive experience during your nightly astral travels, you need to have definite goals, even destinations. The following list will help you to choose a positive goal.

1. Meeting with an appropriate teacher-guide for help in solving current problems.

2. Studying spiritual knowledge in astral classes.

3. Visiting with physically deceased loved ones and friends.

4. Taking a look at a past life. Use this to check on the causes of present problems and/or illnesses.

5. Looking into your own future. This is useful in checking for upcoming problems or obstacles.

6. Asking to receive prophecies connected with future events, such as the safety of a plane for travel, the possibility of an earthquake in a specific area, etc.

7. Working healing or magick on the astral for yourself or others.

8. Visiting a present area of the world you always wanted to see but can't afford to visit.

9. Meeting with another particular astral traveler, usually for the purpose of influencing the person in one way or another.

The last two items listed obviously can be opened to negative uses. Visiting a present place can be perverted into industrial spying if one is good enough at astral travel and can recall at will all the details seen. There are magickal ways to counteract this type of intrusion, though; these will be explained in Chapter 11.

Influencing another person can become unethical, depending upon your motives. If you are trying, for example, to manipulate someone into loaning you money, give in to your sexual advances, or make you heir to her/his estate, then you had better reconsider. The other person's astral aura and determination may be stronger than yours. In this case, you will likely return with a physical headache and a depleted and/or ruptured aura. An aura in this condition allows intrusion of negative thought-forms into your life; these can create anything from illnesses to a run of bad luck.

If, however, you are trying to influence your child to do better in school, give up the bad influences of certain friends, break a cycle of bed-wetting or nightmares, then I say, pull out all the stops and have at it. As a concerned parent, you have every right to try to help. But be certain your motives are positive, and that you present the situation in a positive attitude while out on the astral. If you go at it from a "you will do as I say" position, you will very likely get a "I'll do the opposite" reply.

In order for this deliberate astral meeting to work properly, you have to be able to visualize the person's face clearly in your mind as you go to sleep.

This type of positive confrontation on the astral is also useful when preparing for a job interview, making an offer on property, or trying to resolve a relationship issue. In the job interview, you can visit your prospective employer and ask that she/he give you a fair evaluation for the position. You can tell a prospective seller what you feel is a fair price and ask her or him to be open to the proposal.

In relationships, this astral interview can become tricky, especially if you don't prepare yourself for all possibilities. Marilyn and her husband were not getting along, and hadn't been for some time. She knew he had another relationship going, but would be vindictive if she mentioned divorce. Every night for about two weeks, Marilyn went onto the astral and tried to reason with her husband to mend the marriage. His physical reaction was to become more hostile and remote. Finally, she began to appeal to his more selfish side, assuring him that an equitable divorce would leave him free to do whatever he wanted, that she was merely a hindrance. Within a week, he brought up the subject of divorce himself, offering a fair settlement. He even offered to pay for further schooling for her.

Many of your astral experiences may be cloaked in symbolism because the conscious mind is trying to control the situation. No dream book will be of help in these instances. You need to keep an astral-dream journal where you record all these remembered experiences, no matter how bizarre they seem. Repetition of certain scenes, symbols, or events may point to something of importance for you. You need to contemplate these and also ask your teachers for assistance in interpretation. Symbols seldom mean the same thing to more than one person. Symbols tend to

be individualized through past life experiences. You must discover much of their meaning for you through contemplation and looking truthfully at your previous incarnations.

Five

Bi-Location

You may not be familiar with the term "bi-location." However, you probably have read or heard about the double, fetch, or doppelganger. This last word came into prominence during medieval times in Europe. In India, it is called the *linga sharirah* or *Kama Rupa;* the French knew it as the *perisprit.* The ancient Norse legends speak of the *Scin Laeca* (shining body), an exact duplicate of a person who was surrounded by a ghostly light. The fact that this part of the astral body is an exact duplicate promoted the term "double."

The Scottish Celts call this twin shadow a *coimimeadh,* or Co-walker. Robert Kirk, in his treatise written in 1690 or 1691, said that this companion of each person was often seen by others when the individual was not there. By sighting this Co-walker, people knew that someone would come for a visit or was dying. The Scots believed that this shadow-person was a guardian sent by the faeries. If another person was sincere and asked this Co-walker to communicate with her/him, it would do so. However, communication was considered to be difficult in most cases, if not impossible.

This astral form can sometimes be physically seen at one location while the person is in another. Thus, the expression of bi-location, or two places at once. There are many records of such incidents.

The person whose double is "out and about" may or may not be aware of what is happening. The term "fetch" came into use when it was understood that this double could fetch back information. Usually the person whose double is projected to another location is, or has been, concentrating and desiring to see the person to whom the double appeared.

Ordinarily this astral double is seated very close to the physical body. For those who can see auras, it can appear as an extremely thin, dark line that conforms exactly to the body and lies touching it. It is the innermost part of the aura. Through physical shock, spontaneous projection, or deliberate control, this form can be sent to a location, bearing a message or checking on something, while the person to whom it belongs goes about his or her regular activities.

During World War II, several of my mother's brothers, cousins, and other relatives were in one branch or another of the military. Her youngest brother, Leonard, was on a ship in the Pacific in the midst of some of the heaviest fighting. He hadn't been allowed to come home for Grandma's funeral and was quite upset about everything at home. His letters were few and usually most of the writing was cut away by censors. One sister, Viola, was in the Army stationed in California where she helped test refitted B52 bombers before the planes were sent back into action.

I was five years old and just learning to keep my mouth shut about things I "saw." It was a sunny day during canning season. My mother stood at the sink peeling fruit when an audible tapping came on the kitchen window. Leonard stood outside, smiling. She ran outside, thinking he had come home on leave without telling anyone. Of course, no one was physically there. I knew he wasn't real because I could see through him. A few days later word came that Aunt Viola had been killed in a plane crash while testing a bomber. When Leonard came home, he told my mother he knew something terrible was wrong and lay on his bunk that day thinking how much he wanted to see Viola and her.

This is a classic case of unknowingly projecting the astral double because of intense desire. The same thing can happen during surgery, accidents, and childbirth.

When the astral double travels, your conscious realization does not go along with it. If you know how to send out your double, and do this on a regular basis, this type of projection can become automatic in nature. The double returns to transmit its information in a different fashion than in regular astral travel. The double sends its information through the subconscious mind; this then surfaces in the conscious mind as intuitive thoughts.

To project the astral double, sit in a light meditative state and, with a definite goal in mind, visualize your double standing before you. Then give it instructions on where you want it to go and what you want it to do. Give it a return time so you will know when to communicate with it. You make no attempt to go with it or to loose your astral body at all. When you have given the instructions and sent the double on its way, come out of the meditative state and return to your regular work. When the scheduled return time is near, go once more into the light meditative state, accept the astral double back into your aura, and wait for the information to surface in your mind. You may need to involve yourself in some repetitive work for the conscious mind to lose its hold on the subconscious enough for the information to be made available.

If you have difficulty getting the astral double to project, you may want to try closing your eyes and looking upward at the center of your forehead. This is the location of the pineal gland, the brow center, and what is called the third eye. Ancient Indian Vedic texts say that this area contains the highest and most powerful source of ethereal energy available to humans.

Sending the astral double when you haven't the time or privacy to astral project totally is useful in checking on the safety of loved ones and friends, attending meetings or lectures, or sending and receiving messages from other psychics.

Gwyn was concerned about her daughter driving home late one night from college classes, so she sent out her double to check. She went back to her kitchen cleaning and waited for its return. The message said all was well. When Julie came home, she was shaking all over. "You know that intersection at the college?" Julie said. "Well, I was tired and not paying attention like I should. All at once, I saw you in front of the car shouting to stop. I slammed on my brakes, just as a car ran the stop light. If I hadn't seen you and stopped, he would have hit me."

Sending messages in this manner is common between psychics who know each other well. Most of this communication is put down as telepathy by those who don't understand or believe in the astral double. With telepathy, the messages simply materialize in the mind. However, there is a distinct feeling in the room when a double arrives; the same feeling occurs when someone totally astral projects, but the sensation is stronger. You suddenly get the feeling that you are not alone.

If the projected double is from someone you know and like, you may simply think that a friend walked in without your being aware. If it is from someone you don't know or don't like, then the sensation is uncomfortable.

If you are comfortable with the double, sit down quietly and allow your mind to receive the message. You can also send a return message if you want. However, if you are uncomfortable, the best thing to do is tell the double to leave. Do this in a firm tone of voice; trace a pentagram in the air between you and it if it doesn't leave immediately. If you are at work or in a place where these actions would cause comment, give the command and trace the pentagram in your mind. See that pentagram glow with power. Nothing astral can harm you unless you give it permission to enter your aura or are afraid, which in turn creates an opening in your aura.

If you get the distinct feeling that someone, through her/his astral double, is snooping and spying on you, magickal defenses need to be erected. Chapter 12 goes into this in detail.

You need practice and patience when learning how to send out the double and receive its messages upon its return. Choose a time when and person with whom the details can be confirmed later. If you practice with a sense of fun, you are more likely to get results than if you are tensely determined. Remember, fear, stress, and tension all work against you in any type of astral projection.

Six

Time
Travel

The concept of time is a human invention for the convenience of dating activities and events. On the astral plane, time is looked at in a totally different way. It is possible to delve through any section of time, past, present, or future, when in the astral body. Psychics have learned how to do this to gain the information they need for predictions.

To the subconscious and superconscious minds, however, all time is *now*. These areas of the mind don't understand or accept the human-made concept; to them it is false. Therefore, they have absolutely no problems journeying into the past or the future.

When working with time on the astral planes, the traveler should be aware of certain rules. Whatever events have occurred in the past are rigid. That is, they cannot be changed. Past history of an individual, a culture, or the world can be read with great accuracy as there are no potential possibilities to take into account. But it cannot be changed in any way.

The present area of time can be both flexible and rigid. Some decisions have already been made and there is very little likelihood that they will be changed. Other decisions are in the making. The unset or flexible events can be influenced to change one direction or the other. The more individuals involved in the decision or event, however, the more possibility for last-minute changes of mind.

Events in future times, those things which have not happened yet, become firmer as the time of the event draws closer and becomes the present. The further into the future they are, the more elastic they become. Humans have free will in shaping the future, no matter how clumsy we are most of the time. If enough people actually believe that some catastrophe will occur at a future date, that event will surely come to pass. Psychics and predictors have a responsibility to take care about being doom-and-gloom prophets for this very reason: they encourage people to create the disaster they predicted.

With patience and practice, it is possible for the astral traveler to dip into all these areas of so-called time. Again, one should have a valid reason and/or destination when traveling through time, just as one should have a goal anytime when deliberately journeying in the astral planes.

Some people simply like to go back and view periods of history in which they are interested. Granted, it's a lot more fun than reading a book, especially when so much of what we call history is an agreed upon set of lies. "Facts" have been rewritten so many times by various religious and political factions that you hardly dare take any written history for truth anymore.

Civilizations that have been forgotten or are barely known can be explored in depth while time traveling. The most popular destinations in this category are Atlantis and Lemuria. I think this fascination comes from so many of the present Pagan people having lived in one of those cultures at one period or another. However, there are thousands of other cultures about which we know little or nothing today. The matriarchal society of Catal Huyuk in Turkey, that went 1500 years without war, is a blank to archaeologists except for its beautiful ruins.

When you decide to travel through the past, you need to find markers (certain known events or historical figures) by which you can find your way at first. The best way to do this is by starting with a period of history with which you have some familiarity. You might try delving into your early childhood of this lifetime before going further back. This will give you a feel for finding specific markers and orienting your travels by them. Your teacher-guides can be of great help to you in this type of astral travel, if you ask them to accompany you as "travel guides."

There are five easy methods that will help you with your time travel during meditation or other methods of astral travel. All these methods are symbolic pictures sent to your subconscious mind so that it can understand what you want to do. One method is stepping into the time-river itself; the second is use of the time-tunnel; the third is seeing one door with a time-dial on it; the fourth is using a series of doors; the fifth is the time machine.

The Time-River

Stepping into the time-river is probably difficult for beginners as it requires good astral "sight." You must be able to "see" what is occurring in the mirror of the river and understand what you are seeing. You also have to be able to make a quick decision about stepping into the river. If you vacillate over a scene because you can't make up your mind, you will have to wait patiently until that particular scene appears again. However, if you just want to enter a general period of history in a particular culture about which you know too little to pinpoint an exact time, this is a fun way to get a "surprise" tour.

To use the time-river method, go into a meditative state as you usually do. After dumping your problems, visualize yourself standing on a bank at the side of a smoothly flowing river, staring down into the water below. The surface of the time-river is as smooth as a sheet of glass. As you gaze into the water, you see that this smooth surface contains moving images. If you listen closely, you will be able to hear faint sounds coming to you from this history-reflection.

As you continue to watch the scenes out of history drifting past you, it becomes apparent that culture after culture, century after century, is mirrored here. Soon you see an era of a specific culture that you would like to investigate. Quickly you step off the bank and into the time-river. You do not sink into water. Rather, you sink into the scene you chose, becoming part of it.

You can explore through this time scene as long as you want. You may participate or sight-see like a tourist. The choice is yours. When you are ready to return, think of the river bank and once more find yourself outside the stream of time. To return to your physical body, merely surround yourself with white light and slide back into your body.

The Time-Tunnel

The time-tunnel requires knowing exactly what culture and time period you wish to enter. You travel down a tunnel in the Earth which reaches from your present time to the desired time in history you wish to see. This method works quite well after you have been to a point in history to which you want to return.

Before entering your meditation, decide upon the historical period you wish to visit, preferably one dealing with a past life. Go into your meditation as usual. After dumping your problems, visualize yourself standing before a very high cliff-face with patches of brush and trees along the bottom. In the shadow of a clump of bushes, you spot a narrow cave opening. You squeeze through and find yourself in a large tunnel.

You can see clearly in this tunnel, for the rocks themselves give off a soft glow. You make your way along the smooth tunnel floor winding through the mountainside until you come to an elaborate curtain covering its end. Pay close attention to any symbols on this curtain for they will have meaning for you, as will the predominant color. On the other side of the curtain will be a past life that is important to you and has influence on your present life. Lift the curtain and go through to explore.

When you wish to end the meditation, surround yourself with the white light, think of your physical body, and slide back into it.

The Hall of a Thousand Doors

Using the visual image of a hallway with thousands of marked doors allows you to browse at your own speed. Choose a door, then open it to see what is going on. If you don't like what you see, you can close the door and choose another one.

Go into your meditation as usual through the dumping of your problems. Visualize yourself walking along a path across a meadow. Ahead of you is a high brick wall with a gate surrounding a garden. You reach the beautiful gate which opens at your touch. Once inside, the gate closes behind you, and you see one of your teachers waiting for you.

Together you walk through the garden until you come to a building sitting by itself, surrounded by vast beds of tulips and daffodils. Over the carved entrance is a sign that reads, "Hall of a Thousand Doors."

Your teacher walks with you up to the door, then gives you a blessing and tells you that you must go in alone. You enter and find yourself in a very long hall with doors on each side. The hallway with its many doors goes on and on until you can't see the end.

On each door is the name of a country or a civilization, past, present, or future. You may walk down this hall until you find a door that interests you. If you open the door and don't feel comfortable with what you see, close it and choose another. When you find a scene you like, go through the door. You will find yourself in that time and place. If you decide that you want to try another door, for whatever reason, you have only to look for the door (it will appear to you), go back through it into the hall, and choose another door.

To end the meditation, call upon the white light, think of your body, and slide back into it.

The Time-Dial Door

The door with the time-dial requires that you know exactly where and when you want to go. You can still change your mind if the open door reveals something you would rather not participate in.

During your meditation, go back to the walled garden. One of your teachers will be waiting for you. Together you go to a small marble building with columns across the front. After talking for a while with your teacher, you enter the building alone. There is nothing in the small room inside except a rose-veined marble bench and a door across from you. You walk up to the door and see in its center a large dial. As you turn the dial, you can see small scenes from history appear around its edges. Turn it to the era you want, open the door, and step through.

You are free to explore this historical scene in any way you wish. When you want to end the visit, think of the door and it will reappear. Open it and walk through into the little room. Return to your body in the usual manner.

The Time Machine

The time machine is another way to symbolize to your subconscious mind that you wish to travel through time and space. Before starting your meditation, determine what era you wish to visit: past, present, or future. You can even choose to visit times and places beyond this world. The universe has been and is full of civilizations totally unknown to us at this point. Don't feel limited to the Earth alone.

Go into your meditative state in the usual manner. After dumping your problems, see yourself standing in a room full of electronic equipment. One of your teachers is waiting for you. Take time to talk with this teacher; she/he may suggest places to visit other than the one you have chosen. Tell this teacher where you would like to go, the place and perhaps the time era. Your teacher sets several dials on the electronic equipment and tells you to enter a small booth nearby.

When you are safely inside the booth, the door closes. Over the door are two lights: one red and one green. The red light comes on. In a few moments the red light goes out, the green light comes on, and the door to the booth opens. You are now in the time and place you requested.

You can explore this place as long as you wish. When you are ready to return, re-enter the booth and you will be returned to the room where your teacher awaits. You can discuss any of your travels with this teacher before returning to your body in the usual manner.

You should be aware that if you choose to investigate your own past, you may well find yourself participating in the action rather than watching it. You can always participate while astral traveling, if you want, even though you may not have ever lived in that culture or time period. However, chances of being drawn into the action increase greatly if you enter a door to one of your own past lives.

Since all cultures and time periods of the Earth have known a number of wars and violent conflicts, you should prepare yourself for seeing this first-hand. There is nothing romantic about killing and dying, for whatever reason. Perhaps if more people reviewed the violent periods of history through astral travel, we would be less likely to repeat these costly and painful mistakes. I say this from a spiritual point of view, knowing full well that a great many of those individuals who enjoyed killing and harming others in past lives will willingly be drawn to view these scenes. These particular people, who intentionally locked themselves into a repeating pattern of violence life after life, will be prone to create a similar environment this time also.

Sometimes having a guided meditation or description for astral travel into a particular culture or time period is helpful in the beginning. This helps the traveler to find the markers necessary to determine if you are in the right place. After several visits in this way, you will find yourself going off on your own and having wonderful experiences. This is only right and natural. None of the meditations or guided "tours" are meant in any way to control or limit the traveler. Feel free to experience whatever comes up during such a meditation-travel, even though it may not follow what I have written.

The following historical scenes are based upon what I personally have seen and experienced during deep meditations and astral travel. Use them as guides or markers in the beginning, but be prepared for your experiences to be different as you progress in your astral traveling.

Atlantis

Enter your meditation as usual. Be sure you dump your problems to avoid taking along any negative thoughts.

See yourself standing in a great ancient city. This is part of the continent of Atlantis. Although the buildings are of an ancient type, there are many marvelous things that seem out of the future. The people seem quite ordinary and are of a variety of racial types. Overhead are different types of air-travel machines. The buildings are heated and lighted.

As you draw near a vast complex of acres and acres of large buildings, you must pass through gates in three walls. The central portion of this area is occupied by a beautiful white and gold building that is the Atlantean worship center.

Once inside the third wall, you find that the people there wear insignia on their clothing. These insignia identify their fields of occupation in healing, teaching, philosophy, history, industry, records, medicine, mechanics, and so forth.

You may stop one of these people and ask directions to a certain building which houses something of interest to you, or you may wander about on your own, exploring this beautiful area. Any memories of this region which are important to you will come flooding back.

When you are ready to return, surround yourself with white light and think of your body. You will slide back into it with ease and comfort.

Your exact experiences in Atlantis will depend upon what era you find yourself in. The later historical eras of this culture were corrupt in many areas of government and religion. Many of the priests and scientists had begun unethical experimentations, many of them outright evil. If you find yourself in with these types of Atlanteans, carefully observe, then remove yourself from their vicinity. There were other Atlantean priests, scientists, and people who were opposed to this behavior and can supply you with positive information.

A Tibetan Monastery

Prepare for meditation as usual. Then see yourself standing on a dusty road leading to a high mountain. You can see an ancient stone Tibetan monastery high on the mountainside. Travelers in their dusty cloaks and monks in yellow and orange robes are coming and going on the road. You are on a pilgrimage to the monastery in search of past lives and enlightenment. The memories of any past lives in this region which were important to you will come flooding back.

You begin the last part of your journey up the road to the great doors of the monastery. Full of anticipation, you reach the wooden doors of the temple. You knock and are admitted by a monk. You enter and find yourself in a large entry hall. Leading off are long passageways connecting this room to other parts of the monastery. Wooden doors line the stone walls. There are libraries and meditation chambers, classrooms and healing areas.

Deep in the monastery is a great assembly chamber where prayer and meditation are held. The scent of incense drifts down the halls, and you can hear the sounds of chanting, the faint thud of drums, and the click and whir of prayer wheels.

One of the monks will take you wherever you would like to go. Try to arrange your visit so that you end by going to the assembly chamber and witnessing part of the beautiful ceremonies. When you want to return to your body, follow the usual procedures.

Early in my astral travels, I worked with a Tibetan healing and teaching monk who always wore a natural white robe. This was confusing since all I had read told me that monks wore red or yellow. When I questioned him about this, he would simply smile and say, "Not important you know now." This was very frustrating, but since he knew so much, I forgot about the white robe and learned all I could. Any time I visited the monastery (he called it a lamasery), it was like being a guest. He took me to rooms, chapels, and libraries I would never have found on my own. Later I discovered information stating that there was a certain small branch of monks who did wear white.

Ancient Egyptian Temple

Enter meditation with the usual preparations. Then see yourself on a road in the desert. Around you is shimmering sand. You are part of a caravan heading toward brilliant white buildings you can see before you. Heat waves rise from the sand, and the melodic tinkle of camel bells is all around you.

At last you enter the cool green of the city oasis and pass through the streets to the marketplace. There you leave the caravan and explore the stalls of the merchants. The most wonderful and exciting crafts are on display here.

Finally, you turn into a wider avenue which leads directly to a complex of temple buildings. This avenue is paved with white stone and leads between rows of palm trees and statues.

You walk along this avenue, taking in the sights, until you stand before the great temples. The scent of incense drifts through the air. A faint sound of music and voices reaches your ears. You can enter any temple you wish. You may watch the ceremony and may be allowed to participate. Talk to anyone you wish. Any memories of this region which are important to you will come flooding back.

Return to your physical body and end the meditation in the usual manner.

Some people have a distinct aversion to anything Egyptian. If you fall into this category, don't bypass this astral-meditation but try to discover why you feel this way. Intense feelings, positive or negative, about a culture is a signal that you have lived there.

Early America

Go through your usual meditative procedure. You find yourself in the wilderness of early America. You are standing beside a clearing in a forest. A rutted road leads from one side of the clearing, across it, and through the forest beyond. Not too far ahead of you are several covered wagons. Men on foot and on horseback accompany the wagons.

You now have several choices for exploring this time period. You may go forward and travel with the people in the wagons, or you may visit with any of the Native American groups in the area. You will be able to find and talk with any mountain men and trappers nearby, or you can explore the daily life of some of the small family settlements. If none of these appeal to you, you can go into some of the more settled towns and look at that lifestyle. Any memories of this region which are important to you will come flooding back.

When you are finished with your visit, return to your physical body in the usual manner.

I've never felt any connection with frontier towns, but I enjoyed visiting one of the saloons and seeing first-hand what went on. It was a very unromantic eye-opener, but interesting. It was about this time that my psychic sense of smell kicked in. I had never fully realized before that regular bathing wasn't an important part of many cultures, including our own, until recent times.

After going through your usual meditation steps, see and feel yourself going backward rapidly through time until you reach the ancient civilization of Lemuria.

You are standing on the marble-paved streets of what appears to be a great city set within a park with rolling hills. You begin walking along one of the streets. There are many people moving about who will talk with you if you wish.

The city seems to end abruptly at the edge of a vast forest of redwood and fir trees, but small hills appear among the trees, and the streets narrow but continue through the forests.

As you look closer, you see that the small hills are really the roofs of houses—houses that are built mostly underground but with the front walls exposed for light and a view of nature. Gardens of vegetables, flowers, and exotic shrubs are planted on top of some of the houses.

Behind you, not too far away in the distance, you can see the ocean with docks and buildings along its edge. The markets and trading centers are along this seacoast area. Any memories of this region which are important to you will come flooding back.

As you walk along, many people greet you, and finally one person stops and offers to accompany you as a guide. This person tells you that there are healing centers, temples, learning centers, and shops where art works of all descriptions are made. You may visit people who are responsible for the maintenance of various kinds of power for lighting and other purposes, or you can visit those who handle transportation. Your guide will even take you farther out into the countryside if you wish.

When you are finished exploring Lemuria, return to your body in the usual manner.

Lemuria seems to have been as different from the Atlantean culture as the East is from Europe. I've yet to discover any libraries, but there were teaching areas.

The Sacred Temple at Karnak

Go through the meditation steps in your usual manner. You are on an Egyptian boat on the Nile River. It is a beautiful day. A little breeze now and then fills the white sails, and the sailors help by pulling at the oars. You lean against the wooden railing and watch the villages and people along the banks of the river. Any memories of this region which are important to you will come flooding back.

The boat travels past the cities of Coptos and Kus and Nagadah, until you are in the long westward stretch of the River Nile. Ahead of you, red in the sunset, rise the walls of the city of Thebes. Soon you see many boats tied up in the harbor there for the night before either going on up the river or across to the great temples of Karnak and Luxor.

Your boat crosses the river to the stone dock before the massive temples of Karnak. Gold-tipped flagstaffs before the painted pylons bear scarlet banners that flutter in the evening breeze.

You disembark onto the stone pier and a guide from one of the temples meets you. Together you walk up the stone-paved avenue toward a high wall that surrounds the spectacular temple of Amen-Ra. The guide tells you that the series of temple buildings stretches for nearly a quarter of a mile.

You pass through a gateway flanked by two towering, slim square obelisks. Their surfaces are covered with inscriptions. Beyond the gate and leading into the temple is a colonnaded court, followed by another hall containing massive columns. The walls, columns, ceilings—every surface exposed to the eye—are covered with sculptures of deities, heroes, and hieroglyphs, painted in vivid colors.

Beyond this last hall is the shrine of Amen-Ra, the dwelling place of the god. This rectangular, windowless room contains a statue of the god seated on a throne and wearing as a headdress a kind of crown with two straight, tall plumes.

Nearby, in the temple complex, are other shrines to other gods and goddesses. Surrounding the shrines are storerooms, offices, and living quarters for the priests and priestesses. Your

71

guide tells you that just outside the main building is a sacred lake with another smaller temple beside it.

You are free to explore and witness or take part in many of the ceremonies. You can talk with the priests and priestesses. If you wish, you can go back across the river and explore the city of Thebes.

When you are finished exploring, return to your physical body in the usual way.

If you wander around enough, you will find the ordinary life that existed beyond the temple ceremonies. Once I found myself pressed into counting jars of oil and dates in a storage room. It seems one of the stewards was getting a kick-back from one of the deliverers of food; he was declaring more food delivered than actually was.

The Mystery School at Dodona

After going through your usual preparation steps in meditation, see yourself in Epirus in the northern part of ancient Greece. There are rugged, rocky mountains all around, except for the brilliant blue sea behind you and occasional groves of trees scattered over the landscape. You follow a well-traveled dirt road toward a rocky mountain pass. Once through the pass, you find yourself in a narrow valley surrounded by mountains. Ahead, you can see a large grove of trees. The sun is very warm in a clear sky. Among the trees in the grove ahead is the gleam of white buildings.

Finally, you are walking under the shade of the great oak trees. Some of them are very ancient, their trunks gnarled and twisted. This is a famous Mystery school, Dodona, for training of psychics and prophets. Any memories of this region which are important to you will come flooding back.

There are many white buildings here, glistening in the bright Aegean sunlight. The main complex of buildings is set on three sides of a rectangular courtyard. The largest building is the main temple. Other buildings are a library, a gymnasium, an open-air theater, and living quarters for the lower priestesses and students.

A priestess greets you. You walk with her toward the main temple. You join other priestesses and students who are going into the temple for a ceremony. Inside is a shrine to Zeus and one to Diana. Your guide tells you that the private rooms of the chief priestesses adjoin this temple. You can hear wind chimes, tinkling fountains, and the voice of the wind through the great groves of trees. The ceremony begins.

When the ceremony is finished, everyone goes back to their classes or to meditate under the ancient trees. You can feel the great energy flowing up out of the ground itself. This is an excellent opportunity to take part in other ceremonies, listen in on classes, or to talk with the priestesses. If you wish, your guide will take you to one of the psychics for a reading before you leave Dodona.

To finish this journey, return to your body in the usual manner.

As with the sacred precinct of Delphi, Dodona first belonged to the Goddess in one of Her many forms. You can also ask for healing within Dodona; they have excellent healers.

The Acropolis at Athens

After going through your usual preparation steps in meditation, you find yourself in the ancient busy city of Athens. From the harbor town that serves it all the way up the great stone-paved walled road to the city proper, which lies at the foot of a high rocky plateau, crowds of people are coming and going. You can see there is a gradual rise on the west side of the plateau, making it easy to reach the gleaming temples on its top. The other three sides of the plateau fall away in rocky cliffs.

As you wander about the streets, you pass many shops with open fronts displaying their wares. Any memories of this region which are important to you will come flooding back.

Finally, you reach the top of the plateau and pass through massive wooden gates. Far below at the base of the hill you can see more temples, theaters, park-like areas, gymnasiums, craft shops, and Athenian homes.

An Athenian citizen stops to talk and tells you that this sacred plateau is called the Acropolis. He tells you of several interesting places to visit in the city below.

You may visit any temple on the Acropolis and/or go back down into the city. In Athens, there are philosophers meeting with their students in the parks and around the gymnasiums. Sculptors and metal-workers have shops there. The theaters are performing Greek plays. There are a variety of shops where the Athenians like to meet and talk: barber shops, perfume mixers and vendors, food merchants, jewelers, and many others. At the docks there are sailors unloading foreign cargoes from their ships.

You are free to come and go as you like. When you are ready to return, call up the white light and slide back into your physical body.

Be prepared for male nudity in the gymnasiums and a few other places. The Greek men considered the male body to be a thing of beauty and weren't the least disturbed by going nude on certain occasions. As I was standing in the marketplace looking at some wonderful pottery, around the corner jogged a group of soldiers in very short tunics. I had forgotten that many ancient people did not wear underwear.

The Ancient Druids

Go through your usual preparation to enter deep meditation. After you dump your problems, see yourself in an ancient Celtic area, such as England, Wales, Ireland, Scotland, or the Continent. There are only dirt roads and paths through the thick forests. These are the days of the early Celtic peoples, the Druid priests and priestesses with their vast knowledge of the universe and the Earth itself. Any memories of this region which are important to you will come flooding back.

You follow one of the paths through the beautiful green forest. It is near dusk on a sunny day. Soon you come to a clearing near a gentle river. There are many wooden huts in the clearing, and people dressed in brightly colored homespun clothing are busy here. One building sits a little apart, and before it stands a tall bearded man dressed in white, waiting for you. He is a Druid priest of a high rank and very knowledgeable.

He greets you by name and welcomes you to his home. You go inside and talk with him for some time. The Druid invites you to go with the clan through the forest to a circle of standing stones where a sunrise ceremony will be held.

When you step outside, it is night. The clan waits with lighted torches, and you go with them through the forest. Soon you come out into an open grassy meadow. Ahead in the fading moonlight is a circle of tall gray stones. Druid priestesses wait beside the circle.

As the priestesses and the Druid priest lead the people into the ring of stones, the first rays of dawn can be seen in the sky. The ceremony is gentle and beautiful. You stand with the Celts, watching as the sun slowly rises above one of the tall stones.

After the ceremony is over, the people of the clan sit in the meadow and share food they brought with them. The sun is up now. Children run and play in the grass. As the clan members go back to their homes, the spiritual leaders invite you to go with them down another path.

Soon you come to a very small clearing surrounded by oak trees, one of which is a very old giant of a tree. There are several small huts here belonging to the priestesses. Wooden benches and small tables sit under the shade of the oak trees. These spiritual leaders gather about you on your bench. They talk to you, telling you many ancient and forgotten mystical secrets.

When you are ready to return, call up the white light and slide back into your physical body.

When a friend, Edna, went through this astral-meditation, she did it with reluctance because she wasn't interested in Druid ceremonies. Just as she got to the stones in the meadow, she heard someone call her name. She was delighted to find a group of faeries beckoning to her. She followed them into the forest and shared a magnificent lunch with them; she described all the food in great detail. This little incident shows that you can always have a wonderful time on the astral if you keep your eyes and ears open.

The Ancient Library at Alexandria

After going through your usual preparation steps in meditation, think of the ancient city of Alexandria, Egypt, and you will swiftly be taken there. The streets are extremely busy and crowded with a variety of people from many cultures. With you is a guide, a fellow pilgrim, who is also going to visit the vast library of Alexandria. Any memories of this region which are important to you will come flooding back.

The two of you decide whether you will ride in a chariot or walk through the busy city. As you go along, you stop at the market places and watch the camel caravans and craftsmen at work.

Finally, you come to a high wall with a closed gate. When you knock at the door, the gatekeeper speaks to you through the barred window. You tell him your name and that you have come to study in the great library. He checks his list and lets you in.

You find yourself in a beautiful park-like garden area. The noise of the city beyond is muffled. You hear the sound of birds and the tinkling music of falling water within this garden.

In the center of this garden stands a huge, magnificent building. Your guide has been here often. She/he tells you that there are almost a million scrolls and records kept here: histories and translations from every country in the world; art objects of all kinds; even records from Atlantis and Lemuria.

The main doors stand open to the garden silence. An older woman, filled with dignity and grace, sits at a table near this door. She is the main librarian. As you approach, she calls you by name and welcomes you.

Inside are many more librarians and learned scholars who can help you find the scrolls and records you seek. They will also answer your questions and help you with any difficulties you may have in reading the information.

When you are ready to return, call up the white light and slide back into your physical body.

The first time or two in the great library you may find it very difficult to understand what is written on the scrolls and records. When you ask for help, you might be told that the information is too difficult for you to understand at this time. Be patient and persevere. Find something you can understand and work your way into the more difficult sections.

The Oracle at Delphi

After going through your usual preparation steps in meditation, you see yourself on an ancient Greek ship, docking in the harbor south of the sacred site of Delphi. The water is a transparent blue, vivid and clear under the hot sun. Any memories of this region which are important to you will come flooding back.

A priest of Apollo waits for you on the dock and leads you up the narrow path to the south slopes of rocky Mount Parnassus. Ahead, you can see a few clusters of trees on the lower rugged slopes. Soon you can see brilliant white buildings shining among the trees.

At last you stand in the shade of the trees near a pool formed by a little stream. Around you are many sizes and shapes of temples. The priest tells you that the Temple of Apollo is a sacred cavern beneath the overhanging cliffs called the Shining Rocks. In preparation for your entrance to this sacred place, you remove your sandals and wash your face, hands, and feet in the stream. You can feel the great psychic energy flowing up from the ground into your body.

You are led to the cave entrance where you are met by more priests. Near this entrance stands a sacrificial brazier where the priests burn laurel leaves and barley meal. They fan this smoke over you for purification.

You tell the priests what question you want answered, and they write it down on a clay tablet. Then one of them leads you down a winding tunnel to the sacred cavern. He opens a door and you find yourself walking into a small cavern. A large golden statue of Apollo shines in the flickering lamplight.

The sacred priestess, Oracle of Apollo, is sitting on a high bronze seat in the center of the room. From a small crack in the rock beneath her chair rise fumes of an exotic odor. Overhead is a tiny crack in the ceiling through which the fumes disappear. The priest lays your tablet on the floor near her chair and waits quietly. The priestess never looks at it.

The Oracle looks at you in silence, then relaxes and goes into a trance. She begins to speak, giving an answer to your question.

When the Oracle has finished, the priest leads you back to the cavern entrance. You may now talk to the priests or visit the other temples.

When you are ready to return, call up the white light and slide back into your physical body.

The Delphic Oracle may give a straight-forward, under-standable answer to your question, but she may also give you the answer in a sort of riddle. Try to remember exactly what she said and write it down. Think about it, even if it seemed to be the non-riddle type. The Delphic Oracle was known for couching her words in such a way that the interpretation could trick you if you weren't careful.

Be prepared to discover that recorded history and what you see of history when you astral travel are not always the same. Recorded history is most often an agreed upon set of lies. Don't reject unrecorded history. There are a tremendous number of events and civilizations about which we know extremely little or nothing. There is no record of them available to us. Be prepared to encounter some civilizations you didn't know existed.

Check into your past lives to discover latent talents, relationship connections, and/or the reasons for continuing problems you may be experiencing. Do you consistently choose the same kinds of friends and lovers who eventually prove to be detrimental to you? Do you have a talent you haven't fully developed yet but which you love? It isn't logical to assume that so-called geniuses like Mozart gained all their talent in one lifetime. However, be brutally truthful when you look at these past lives.

Using astral travel to check the future is like having extra insurance. It is an excellent idea to periodically check your own future, especially if there is an upcoming decision to be made or you have to travel. Don't snoop into the future of others unless their decisions and activities will have a direct effect upon you. If their continued negative influences impinge upon your life, the best solution is to sever the relationship. That's a lot easier and more positive than constantly having to check the future to keep them from sabotaging your life.

You can use the same techniques to astral travel into the future as you did when you traveled into the past. However, it is a little more difficult since you have no pre-set markers to follow. The only way you can establish markers is to concentrate upon the event you wish to see.

Suppose you are planning a trip by plane, train, or car. Naturally, you would check to see if there were any potential disasters involved. If you see any, or feel uneasy, check on alternative routes or methods of transportation. You might even postpone the journey altogether or schedule it for a different date. Remember, the closer an event is to occurring, the more set it is and the less likelihood you have of making changes through the astral. The further you go into the future, the more elastic the outcome.

The same procedure can be applied to decisions you need to make, purchases you want to make, and meetings you want or need to attend. Create changes if you see an unsatisfactory out-come. Whenever it is necessary to be with people when you have foreseen problems, protect yourself and stay away from the possible troublemakers as much as possible. Rethink decisions and purchases. Waiting for a better time may solve the whole thing, or buying a different product or purchasing your chosen product at another store may eliminate any trouble.

Astral traveling into the future takes absolute clear-seeing and lots of patience. If you refuse to face the truth, you will only hurt yourself. You may honestly miss something in future travel, but in general you will catch all the major problems before they arise.

Seven

Visiting in the Here and Now

Astral traveling to see friends or lovers in the present is one way to verify immediately that you actually can astral travel. However, don't measure your success by whether you can accomplish astral travel in this fashion. Some people simply don't seem to have much success in deliberately making present time visits, but they find it easy to time-travel and sleep-travel. Each person is unique in his or her abilities, whatever those abilities are, so don't set your standards of achievement by the achievements of others.

When making present time visits, don't go where you would not be welcome physically. That is an impolite and unethical intrusion. Don't snoop. Besides, you may well find yourself viewing a scene that would be embarrassing if you physically walked in.

If you are trying to check up on a spouse or lover to see if she/he is cheating on you, the intense emotions and fear associated with finding out will probably keep you from seeing the truth or even getting near the person. When you are under emotional stress, you cannot have a detached emotional attitude toward astral travel. It is highly unlikely you will reach the correct destination, if you get out of your body at all.

The best method of astral traveling in the present time is to make arrangements with a sympathetic, understanding friend or acquaintance who is also interested in astral travel and ESP. Arrange to visit on a specific day and time, just as you would for a physical visit. Go into your meditative state and visualize the face of the person you plan to visit. You may or may not feel your astral body going to that location. Keep looking at the face before you. Then project a brief message. Look quickly around the room, if you can see it, and note anything that is different from when you last visited. Return to your physical body.

Compare notes with your receiver when you can. Someone who is very sensitive psychically may be able to see you, but it takes a practiced, strong projector to create a visible astral body that can be seen by others. Perhaps the person didn't get the message, but felt as if someone else was in the room. If the person has pets, those pets could have reacted differently when you were there in the astral. The friend may have received something, but the message may have come through in a garbled state. In these cases, you chose a message that was too long or involved.

If you had no obvious success, don't despair. Often the deliberately willed travel will not occur, but that night or the next you will find yourself, during sleep, where you wanted to go. Tenseness kept the first visit from happening, but when you relaxed during sleep, your astral body did what you wanted it to do. You have to develop an attitude of wanting to astral travel, but not caring if you don't.

Astral travel, whether deliberate or during sleep, can be useful in sending messages. Perhaps you haven't seen someone in quite some time and would like to hear from her/him. You don't know where the person is, so trying to get there through surroundings definition is out. Before going to sleep, picture the person as you last saw her/him. As you hold that picture in your mind, send out a message for the person to call, write, or come to see you. This impresses the need to deliver the message upon the astral body. As soon as you are "out and about," your astral body should deliver your message. If there has been a long period of silence between you and the receiver, you may have to send the message on several occasions.

You can also use this method to contact close or casual acquaintances to pass on information. You might be on a trip and not near a phone; send them word that you are okay. If passing through a friend's town unexpectedly, you can send a message ahead that you will stop for a visit. If you need to call someone and are not sure of the person's schedule, astral visit to obtain the best time.

Don't be a peeping tom. You not only have a responsibility to be ethical about your astral travels, but you can incur a karmic debt by being a snoop. If you snoop, you open the door to being snooped on. Like attracts like. If you feel that some astral traveler is taking this unwarranted liberty with you, build up a barrier that allows only positive energy through. Chapter 12 goes into detail on these magickal procedures for defense.

Perhaps you were guilty of astral snooping in the past, or you had a negative relationship, since broken off, which you feel still gives the other person access to you through the astral. This can be a problem if not properly taken care of. The first thing you must realize is that, for whatever reason and without pointing fingers, you built up negative karma. The choice was yours to become involved in the activity or relationship. You may feel like an idiot because you snooped or allowed yourself to become involved, but if you plan to grow spiritually, you absolutely have to take responsibility for your part in what happened. This goes right back to the saying, "Never teach karma to anyone who is not willing and prepared to overcome it."

I am speaking only of negative karma here; the positive karma we just sit back and enjoy. Many people think that they have to endure negative karma to the bitter end; maybe by going through all the continuing painful consequences they gain the sympathy and subtle control they like. (More on this attitude in Chapter 10 about healing.) Often we find people still paying the penalty long past a reasonable point. Life is too long, in my opinion, to be hampered by old and painful debts, especially when there is no longer a reason to endure them.

If you truthfully want to free yourself from negative karmic debt, this is a time for some serious introspection and truthfulness. Can you see the mistakes you made and did you honestly learn from the experience? This means acknowledging your part in the experience. What was your real motive for doing what you did or being involved?

An example was my first marriage. It was literally hell on Earth. But I married to get away from my mother, who was quite skilled at manipulation, intimidation, and control. All I did was exchange one set of negatives for another. Trying to be truthful with myself, I delved into past lives and discovered a prior connection with this woman. As an aunt in control of my estate, she had been basically the same type of person. I escaped by marrying. I realized she had the opportunity to discharge the debt this time, but refused to take it. I came in knowing the possibilities and repeated the whole thing again. I determined I wasn't going to play that game any longer. I got a divorce and worked hard at keeping that tie severed by not holding a grudge. My mother, I politely but firmly kept at arm's length; I told her nothing of my personal life and allowed her to make no comments or decisions for me. Unfortunately, she never got the message and right up until her death was still trying to manipulate. However, that had nothing to do with me. The emotional ties were cut.

Are others still making you pay for past mistakes? Many times we give others power over us by letting them constantly bring up old issues and mistakes long after we have learned the lesson and made changes. Never share your mistakes with narrow-minded people; they never miss an opportunity to hold them over your head. Don't lie to yourself. Did you really and honestly make the changes or just convince yourself you did? If you honestly made changes, tell others to keep their comments and opinions to themselves.

Are you still making yourself pay? We humans have a bad habit of flogging ourselves for mistakes long past what is necessary. The first step is to forgive yourself for whatever you did and vow not to repeat it. One method that can help in the forgiving is to see one positive thing that came out of the experience. You might have to really search, but the good thing is there. Then you can release the deep emotions that experience caused, which in turn releases you from further karma with the people involved. This should be applied to each negative experience, whether it is an immediate or past event. For this to work, you must reach a state of indifference: no hate, no resentment, no feeling cheated. And you must make every effort *not* to repeat the action.

There is an old saying: "Sharing a sorrow cuts it in half." Don't buy this! Sharing a sorrow (particularly when it was a mistake you made) may make you feel better at the time, but I can assure you that, unless you choose your listener with extreme care, you will have created more problems than you had before. Many people will subconsciously send out aura threads that attach to your aura and, in a manner of speaking, bind you to them. The same applies in reverse with people who go around telling all who will listen about their problems.

This also applies to confessions and going to someone you have wronged with an apology. If something you did or said involved another person in an intense emotional situation, it will be unusual for that person to be detached enough to accept your apology in a positive manner. I'm not saying not to apologize; do it if you can. However, be aware that your very presence and words will stir up old emotions, which can cause auric threads to go between the other person's aura and yours. This applies whether you are in the person's presence in either the physical or the astral body.

There has been a wave of people taking part in what used to be called EST; they've changed the name today. Part of this program requires that the participants apologize to people they have wronged. On the surface, this is positive mental action. It works only if the participant is sincere. I've received such calls from three people in this program. One person was sincere; with one I

85

felt the auric threads trying to attach themselves to my aura by calling up memories; the last person was outright lying and tried to attach the threads by argument.

The quickest and easiest emergency methods for protecting yourself in such a situation you may already do automatically. One method is to cross your arms across your solar plexus area. This center of emotion, or chakra, is where most people try to attach their auric threads. By crossing your arms in this area you are denying the offending person access to that center. The second method is to make three sharp cutting sweeps across the solar plexus to sever any threads that you feel trying to attach. This works particularly well to ward off thoughtforms sent to do the attaching.

You can make your apology in a less dangerous manner by first forgiving yourself, then making positive and permanent changes in your life. After this, send the other person good wishes and keep your emotional thoughts to yourself.

When you are traveling about in the astral, you may get a glance of something in the very immediate present which you want to avoid if at all possible. It doesn't matter if you think it is elastic enough to change or not. At least give it your best try.

Begin by determining why this may be happening. See what you can personally change within yourself to circumvent the coming problem. If it involves an individual who has negative feelings toward you, try to change the person's feelings or erect a barrier. If it involves an unknown individual who plans random harm, see why you would be drawing this type of action and then take precautions. Work on changing the future event so that the individual is caught by the police through her/his own mistakes.

If the event you saw involves a personal relationship or friendship, see whether you are holding onto a situation that is dying or dead. Why are you doing this, or why is it being done to you? Some friendships and relationships are not to your benefit and must be terminated. If it concerns a family member, can you sever or limit communications?

If this upcoming negative event concerns a job, you can put out desires to change employment or move the troublesome person on to a better position that takes her/him away from you.

To create such changes in an upcoming event you have seen approaching while in the astral, go into your usual meditative state. When you are totally relaxed, call up the astral preview of the event. See the event completely through and observe all details: what is said, what is done, all the actions and reactions. Now choose one single aspect of the event and create it in a more positive mode in your mind. Keep working at the change until it sticks. Then go on to another aspect and make changes. It may well be that you will need only to create changes in one or two small aspects to change the vibration of the event.

Don't try to make it go away entirely. You can't do that, for the event is already on its way to happening. You can only influence how it may happen and how you will react to it. Just before you come out of your astral travel, tell your subconscious mind to set warning signals within your aura to keep you alert. Once back in your normal mode of operation, make any changes you have determined will help you to avoid the unpleasantness.

One very rewarding part of astral travel in the present time mode is going to places you can't afford to visit in the physical body. To set the correct markers for such a journey, collect travel folders and read books on the place you wish to visit. The more colored pictures of the area, the better. Find out about all the things you would see if you actually planned a trip to that region. When you go into your deep meditative state, call up a bright colored picture and project yourself there.

That this can actually work was proven to me by an acquaintance who wished to visit the Bahamas but couldn't afford to spend the money to get there. Rita knew how to astral travel while in deep meditation and had achieved some reasonable successes with her experiences. Rita had collected every travel brochure she could find. Finally, she scheduled a week's vacation as usual, then went home to enjoy the Bahamas. Twice a day for thirty minutes Rita went astral traveling to the sunny beaches of the Bahamas. The rest of the day she took care of the list of "need to do" things that builds up when one is holding down a job.

87

When she returned to work, her skin showed the redness of a slight sunburn, an extraordinary thing when it had rained the whole week. I kidded her about using a sunlamp. Rita grinned and said, "No, I astral traveled to the Bahamas and spent my week lying on the beach. I could feel the heat, the breeze off the ocean, everything. I guess I overdid it."

It is entirely possible to go jaunting around the exotic spots of the world without leaving home, suffering travel delays, incurring expenses, or coming down with dysentery from drinking the water. Just be certain you are familiar with your destinations through pictures so you will have travel markers.

As you can see, astral travel in the present time can be used positively or negatively, depending upon the ethics and intentions of the traveler. If you are unethical in your use of astral travel, I won't tell you that you will immediately be blasted for your "sin." But you can be sure that sometime you will pay a penalty of some sort. Like attracts like. Lower your ethics, and you may well find yourself attracting unethical astral entities who can plague you in both the physical and astral planes.

Use your astral travels in a productive, positive manner and you will find that your travels, and physical life, will strengthen and benefit.

Eight

Treading Ancient Paths

It is an interesting experience to travel through time for a visit with a wizard, witch, magician, shaman, or ancient teacher. Never discount the validity of such an experience simply because historical records don't mention the existence of these people or their ceremonies. Many such people worked in secret, either because of persecution or because as initiates they took vows of silence. These vows of silence, such as those we know were taken in the Eleusinian Mysteries of Greece, were so important to the initiates that no details were ever revealed about the ceremonies.

As a guide for such an astral journey, you should first call upon your personal teacher-guides. They will act as guides to the proper place, protectors from any predatory astral entities, and consultants for understanding what you have seen.

89

When you reach a certain stage of your development, your teachers will often allow you to stumble upon a negative-slanted person and/or experience in the astral to teach you to be cautious and aware. They won't let you come to harm, but they may let you experience some scary things before rescuing you. I guarantee that an experience or two of this nature will cure you of wanting to dabble with negative astral energies.

Even if you already know one of your spiritual teachers, the following guided journey will help you meet more teachers. What each guide has to teach you will seldom overlap. They each have their specialty. As your astral experience and spiritual growth expand, you may find yourself with a new teacher added to your group. This is part of the normal spiritual growth cycle.

Meeting Spiritual Teachers and Guides

Prepare yourself as usual for a deep meditation. Surround yourself with the white light, relax your entire body, and dump your problems.

Visualize yourself in a beautiful garden. You can feel the warm sun, hear the birds singing in the trees, and smell the flowers. Through the trees ahead, you see a gleaming marble building. Quickly you move toward it. As you walk up the three steps to the open door of the building, you see several people waiting for you.

Use your astral sight to determine whether these people are male or female, short or tall, dark or fair. Study their clothing. Can you tell their nationality from their dress and facial features? They smile and greet you by your name. You may be told their names right away, or some of the names may remain unknown to you for a time. What do your intuitive feelings tell you about them? Don't expect a famous person. Very few so-called famous people knew much about spiritual pursuits.

They cluster about you in welcome, like friends who have not seen each other for a long time. Spend as much time talking with them as you wish. Each teacher-guide will give you some of her/his personal history so you can understand their positions better. Each specializes in a particular spiritual field, such as healing, ancient history, ancient ceremonies, psychic talents, and so on.

This is a get-acquainted time for all of you. Explain your goals and desires to your teachers and listen carefully to their advice. They may surprise you with predictive tidbits on your future which will make you change or solidify some of your goals and plans.

These teachers may take you into the building to show you fascinating objects or may wander about the garden area, showing you where certain other temples, classrooms, and healing centers are located.

If you feel uncomfortable with any of these teachers, ask them why you feel this way. Check your intuition against their answers. You may just feel uncomfortable with their higher vibrations or because their appearance means you will have to make some heavy personal changes.

On rare occasions, a teacher will appear alone who is not of the high astral level you want. Beings like this are masquerading as something other than they are. If you discover this is so, politely send the entity packing! Yell for help from your other teachers. Your regular teacher-guides may have allowed this imposter to make an appearance as a sort of test.

Sometimes, though, this lone teacher is not "evil" or a low-level entity, but rather inexperienced. Beings like this are similar to student-teachers on this plane, who must go out and learn while teaching. Be polite and patient with these entities. One day you will be a spirit and may well find yourself being someone's teacher-guide.

Many times your teacher-guides will have known you in another lifetime. When they begin helping you to re-discover the memories of the life in which they knew you, it can be like old home week.

When you are ready to leave, your teachers gather around you. Each blesses you and gives you a warm hug. You feel the white light closing around your form and you slide back into your physical body.

This informal type of meeting with your teacher-guides can be repeated whenever you want. It is an excellent way to talk over problems and plans with them. As with all friends, the closer you keep in touch with these spiritual entities, the better the communication and the stronger the friendship.

Now you are ready to consider planning an astral trip to visit a person of the past who practiced some form of magick. Following are four guided astral journeys: to a wizard, a witch, a shaman, and a ceremonial magician. These will enable you to see the differences and similarities in these four forms of magick.

Before undertaking any of these journeys, you need to understand a brief definition of each of these. A wizard, also called a sorcerer or a sage, was a wise man, one skilled in magick. Wizards existed mainly in the Middle Ages of Europe and tended to be loners. They did magick for the sake of magick and often were involved in what is called alchemy (an early form of the sciences). Their practices had nothing directly to do with religion of any form.

Witches have existed in one form or another for centuries. At first they were mostly women who dedicated themselves to the worship of the Goddess and the God of Nature. After Christianity gained control, the term "witch" came to mean anyone who still followed the Old Religions. By this time, both men and women were called witches. The word "Wicca" or "witch" comes from the Anglo-Saxon language and means "wise one." Only in Scotland were male witches called warlocks. Witchcraft was and is both a religion and a magickal system.

The practice of shamanism has been known in almost every culture around the world at one time or another. A shaman can be either male or female. The shaman uses an altered state of consciousness to journey to other worlds (the astral realms) in order to gain knowledge, predict the future, and heal people. The shaman sees all aspects of the universe as interconnected, a network of energy patterns, vibrations, and entities. She/he becomes an intermediary for her/his clan or tribe between the different worlds.

The ceremonial magician was not a follower of any of the Old Religions, rather believing in a Supreme Creator and what are now called angels and demons. Although this system is a very old one, dating from ancient Mesopotamia and Egyptian times, it was widely used during the Medieval era and is still practiced today. Their rituals were merely a pattern-making system for contacting and using matrices of power.

It is a good idea to do each meditative journey, even though you think you might not be interested in one of them. The whole idea behind astral travel is to learn things you can't learn in any other way. You will be surprised at the magickal and spiritual techniques you can learn from watching ancient practices.

In preparation for visiting a wizard, set your mental markers for the journey by visualizing a medieval city and its inhabitants. Use pictures if you can. Sometimes playing a recording of music from that period, especially the folk music, helps.

Visiting With a Wizard

Prepare for your astral journey in the usual way. After dumping your problems, call your teachers and tell them where you want to go. They will guide you to the astral markers which will lead you directly to a wizard.

When you feel the mental markers, you will find yourself on a street in an old European city. You can feel the cobblestones under your feet. Notice the houses and how they are built. The people hurrying past you are dressed in old styles. As you walk down the street, you can smell that the alleys are far from clean.

Soon a small boy approaches and calls your name. When you answer, he says that his master is waiting for you. You follow him as he leads the way down a narrow side street. It is growing dark by this time, and no lamps light the streets.

At a tall, narrow house, squeezed between other houses, the boy knocks on the door. An older man, dressed in a long robe and slippers, opens the door and beckons for you to enter. The boy runs on down the street.

The wizard introduces himself as Emil. His dark hair falls to the shoulders of his black robe. The slippers on his feet are decorated with strange symbols embroidered in gold. He leads the way into a small room where a pot of tea and two cups sit on a little table. A candle lights the dark room. The two of you sit, drinking tea and talking, until the sky outside is completely dark.

The wizard takes up the candle and asks you to follow him to his workroom. Together you climb two flights of narrow stairs to the very top of the house. There, the wizard unlocks a door and you step into the very private rooms of Emil the wizard.

This room is lined with shelves of old books; the little spaces of bare wall are covered with astrological charts. Hung from the ceiling are dried plants and preserved specimens of various animals, birds, and reptiles. The tables are covered with stones, strange glass bottles and containers, and other interesting things.

You wander around the workroom, asking the wizard to explain things that interest you. Finally, he steps to the table and begins work on a magickal experiment. You watch closely. Emil explains that he is trying to make a magickal mirror that will reflect the images of faeries, gnomes, and elves and help him to communicate with them.

On the table before him is a small, round mirror, its frame covered with strange glowing symbols. The wizard carefully measures out several dried herbs into a mortar and pestle. As he grinds these herbs into a powder, he chants. Then he pours water from a decanter into the bowl and mixes the herbs and water into a thick paste. He spreads this paste evenly over the surface of the mirror as he again chants.

Taking a cloth, Emil carefully wipes off the herb-paste, then cleans the mirror with more of the water. He holds up the mirror to look into its surface and cries, "Look!"

As you look over the wizard's shoulder, you can see, reflected in the mirror, a very small being in the glass. It appears to be sitting on the wizard's shoulder. When you look at Emil's shoulder there is nothing, but when you turn back to the magick mirror you can clearly see the faery. Emil speaks to the faery and its voice comes from the mirror.

With a smile, Emil hands you the mirror. You are fascinated to see a similar entity close to you. As you turn the mirror to reflect various parts of the room, you see several different kinds of little beings. You can communicate with them through the mirror.

You return the magick mirror to the wizard and thank him. When you are ready to return, call to your teachers and they will take you to the garden. There you can discuss the journey and your experience with them. When it is time to return to the physical world, call up the white light and slide through it into your physical body.

Make notes of your journey upon your return. This not only helps you to remember certain things that happened, it strengthens the markers which will help you to return easily for another visit.

Before you take the astral journey to visit with a witch, you need to be certain you are not subconsciously visualizing a false image. Many people do not understand the truth behind Witchcraft and witches. Their minds are cluttered with false propaganda about what a witch really is. Followers of Witchcraft, or Wicca, do not believe in the Christian devil; they don't worship this entity or perform evil rituals. Witchcraft and Satanism are two completely different types of beliefs; they have absolutely nothing in common, except in the narrow minds of certain people.

Witches are not, and never were, ugly old hags cackling over boiling cauldrons. They were and are ordinary men and women who love the Goddess and Her woodland consort. It is highly unlikely that ancient witches celebrated and danced outdoors in the nude. Damp weather, brambles, and unexpected hedgehogs can be very uncomfortable. Witches may be different, but they aren't stupid.

Your first astral journey to a Wiccan coven meeting may follow the guided description. However, if you return, you may find that you encounter different seasons and ceremonies. Keep an open mind and enjoy the power drawn into the circle.

Go into meditation in the usual manner. After dumping your problems, go to the garden and discuss your proposed journey with your teachers. Accept their reassurances that you will be safe at all times and will have a wonderful trip.

As you move out on your journey, you feel the mental markers which guide you into the English countryside of the 1400s. You find yourself near a small cottage. A Full Moon hangs low in the darkening summer sky. As you walk along the dirt path to the cottage, you can smell the rich scent of herbs growing nearby. You knock on the door. A young man opens the cottage door with a smile and bids you enter.

The room is small, with a fireplace at one end. Near the low fire lies an old dog, asleep. A purring calico cat rubs around your legs. A young woman is putting thick slices of bread and meat wrapped in a napkin into a woven basket.

The man introduces himself as John and the woman as Elspeth. He invites you to go with them to their coven meeting. They each put on a dark cloak and offer one to you. John says that the night will be chilly before the meeting is over.

Elspeth takes up the basket and her broom, John his walking staff, and the three of you go out into the night. You follow the dirt road for only a short distance before John leads the way through the roadside grass and into a thick grove of trees. In the bright moonlight coming down through the leaves you can see that John is following a narrow deer path. Quickly the three of you move silently through the forest. Ahead you catch a glimpse of a twinkle of firelight.

Soon the three of you step out into a small forest clearing. In the center is a low fire; overhead hangs the Full Moon in the dark sky. The ground has been cleared of all brush right up to the tall trees. Around the clearing stand several other men and women. "Merry meet," they call, and John and Elspeth answer the same.

Setting her food basket aside, Elspeth and the other women begin to sweep the circle with their brooms. They sweep from the center outward while chanting. When they are finished, everyone gathers near the fire, while one of the older women traces a circle around the clearing with the handle of her broom. She is followed by one of the men, who repeats her action with his staff.

The priestess and priest go to each of the four directions and call upon spirits to guard and protect them. The coven gathers in a circle, alternating men and women, with the priestess in the center. The priestess raises her arms to the Moon and calls upon the Goddess. The people of the coven join hands and dance clockwise around the circle while they sing.

You feel power begin to build within the turning circle. It seems to flow up through your feet, into your body, then around the circle from person to person. The people dance faster until the priestess gives a shout and everyone sinks to the ground.

You can see a glow around the priestess. She seems to transform into another being, one filled with love and power. The priest joins her, his face also transformed.

"The Goddess is with her," your neighbor whispers, "as the God is with him."

You notice the bright eyes of deer and small animals peering out of the forest.

The priest and priestess began to prophecy by turns. They give each person in the circle a message and a blessing. Then the priestess kisses each man, the priest each woman.

One of the witches calls out a name for healing. The coven begins to chant, their hands held with palms toward the priest and priestess. The leaders hold their hands out in the direction of the absent person who needs healing. You feel power flowing through your hands. When it subsides, you find yourself perspiring. The leaders drop their hands and agree that the healing will occur.

The direction guardians are dismissed by those who called them. The priestess and priest cut the circle by swinging their broom and staff across the drawn line.

The food baskets are brought out, and everyone shares the meal. The coven members gather around you, introducing themselves and asking you if you will join them again sometime. One man brings out a small wooden flute and pipes a country dance tune. Several couples dance in the light of the fire.

As you thank John and Elspeth, you feel your teachers drawing you back to the garden. Once there, you talk about your experiences with them. They will answer any questions you have. Then you are ready to return through the light to your physical body.

Shamans were the primary healers of their people, since there was no such thing as a doctor in those times. They learned to produce an altered state of consciousness at will in order to get information needed for healing, hunting, future moves by the clan, and so forth. They were the spiritual guides, but not the physical leaders.

Most people only know of the shamanism practiced by Native Americans, Eskimos, or the Lapps. However, shamanism was at one time an important part of cultures from Mongolia to Ireland. The basics of all types of shamanism are the same, only the details are different.

A shaman is sometimes called a medicine man or witch doctor, depending upon the culture and who is interpreting the ceremony. Among the Mongolian clans, for instance, their words for this person are *buga* and *udagan*. The shamans' primary purposes are and were healing and prophecy for their people.

For the visit to a Mongolian shaman, set your mental markers with the images of hide yurts or tents, herds of horses, and vast areas of rolling grasslands.

The Healing Shaman

Enter your astral meditation as usual. Stop first at the garden and ask your teachers to guide you to the proper place. As you move swiftly through time in the astral realm, you see before you a grassland under a sunny sky. You find yourself astride a wiry little pony heading into a noisy encampment of Mongolian people. Smoky fires of horse dung smolder outside hide tents. Children run, laughing and shouting, among the tents.

Your pony stops before a tent decorated with strange red and black symbols. As you dismount, an old man wearing a cap with bird wings attached steps out of the tent to greet you. He motions for one of the children to care for your pony.

You follow him into the dim tent; a low fire burns in the center of the dirt floor. Inside, you sit cross-legged on a rug while the old man introduces himself. He says your spirits told him that you were coming and would need a healing. At this instant, a young man enters the tent and nods to the shaman.

As the young man takes up a small drum, the shaman tosses a handful of herbs on the smoldering fire. A puff of strange-smelling smoke drifts through the tent. The shaman tells you to lie down on the rug. The assistant begins a steady beat on the drum while the shaman sits beside you, chanting in a low voice. The drumbeat gets faster; the shaman chants louder.

Suddenly he claps his hands over your face, and you feel yourself swirling upward, away from the camp and into another realm of being. The drumbeat merges with your heartbeat. You find yourself in another plane of existence where you meet talking animals and strange, powerful entities. You are not afraid, just curious. These creatures and entities tell you many interesting and important things.

You feel yourself once more swirling away, this time downward into the hide tent. For a moment, you hang near the peak of the tent looking down at yourself and the shaman sitting beside your body. The drumbeat slows, then stops. You and your body merge.

When you sit up, the shaman smiles at you and tells you about your adventures, for he was traveling with you all the time. He reveals to you the importance of the animals who talked to you. If you have any questions about things told to you, the old man will help you understand.

The assistant brings you a rough cup filled with liquid. The shaman encourages you to drink it. The liquid tastes of earth and roots, but you can feel its healing qualities purifying your body, sweeping away all illness.

The shaman puts a small stone into your hand as a talisman, then taps your forehead. You speed away into the astral light. After a short talk with your teachers, you once more go into the light and slide into your physical body.

The ceremonial magicians we are most familiar with existed during the Middle Ages in Europe. They kept their practice secret because of the persecution power of the churches, but called upon angels and demons, a Christian belief. Ceremonial magick was not, and is not, a religious system.

One reason for this astral journey is to give the traveler a feel for the negative entities, without the danger of meeting them unprepared, face to face. One also experiences the beautiful feel of positive entities, called "angels" by the ceremonial magician.

The Magician's Circle

Go into your astral meditative state as usual. Stop to visit your teacher-guides and explain your destination desires to them. They will help you reach the proper destination in the Middle Ages.

You are standing at the door of a country manor house. Around the house you see brick paths leading off through beds of flowers and herbs. You knock and a short, middle-aged man opens the door. He seems to be in a hurry as he invites you in.

He introduces himself as Edmund Warbridge as he leads you to the back of the house and down a flight of stairs to a basement area. This underground space is partitioned off into a small room with a door to another area. There Edmund hands you a robe and tells you to dress in it while he sets up his magickal preparations. He unlocks the other door and disappears inside.

As soon as you are dressed, Edmund opens the door and beckons to you. He is dressed in an elaborate gown. This room has a large circle painted on the floor; around this circle are painted strange symbols and words in some unknown language. Opposite this circle is drawn a large triangle.

The magician positions you within the large circle. He tells you not to leave the safety of this circle no matter what happens. You watch as Edmund draws along the circle edge with a beautiful sword. After this, he carries smoking incense around the area, then sprinkles the edges of the circle with water. He begins to chant in an unknown tongue, the sword held upright in his hand.

The scent of incense is heavy in the closed room. Your skin begins to feel tingly and hot as Edmund points at the triangle with his sword. His words seem to be orders to something you can't see.

A swirling mist begins to gather within the triangle. Dark, angry-looking colors pulse through this mist. At last a form takes shape, a figure that projects an aura of evil and danger. It goes through a series of shapes, taking on the semblance of your worst nightmares. Edmund chants at this entity. Reluctantly, it assumes one form and glares at him. In a deep voice that comes directly from its mind to yours, the entity asks what the magician wants.

Edmund orders it to stop its haunting and troublemaking of a certain house in the village. The entity roars its disapproval and tries to move out of the triangle, but it cannot get loose. Edmund chants again, threatening to bind it in a place of darkness if it does not return to the one who sent it. Finally, the entity agrees, and Edmund dismisses it. It fades away into a wisp of gray vapor.

Edmund turns to you, perspiration on his face. You find that you too are perspiring. The heavy feeling of evil has gone from the room. You know that this spirit was a low-level astral entity.

The magician explains that a magician dabbling in black magick sent the entity to torment the villagers because of some fancied slight. The people of the village think of Edmund as their protector.

"Now I will show you an angel," he says.

Edmund chants again, but does not gesture with his sword. This time the words give off an atmosphere of goodness and light. A brilliant swirl of misty light begins to form in the air above the circle.

A powerful entity begins to form out of the light. This being gives off an atmosphere of peace and love as it looks down upon you. You know that this is an entity from the higher levels of the astral planes.

Edmund looks up at the "angel," intent upon the mental conversation he is having. When the being turns its attention to

101

you, you can clearly hear what it is saying. It speaks to you of your spiritual goals and the plans you have for your future.

Finally, the "angel's" hand briefly brushes Edmund's head in a blessing. Then it reaches for your hand, saying it will return you safely to your teacher-guides. You rise swiftly with this entity and find yourself once more in the astral garden.

You discuss your experiences with your teachers, then return to your physical body in the usual manner.

If you have been strongly in the astral, you will experience a deep sense of repulsion and dread of the low-level entity. The atmosphere such beings carry with them cannot be mistaken for any higher astral being. By experiencing this type of being while in the safety of the ceremonial magician's circle, you can learn to detect and avoid such creatures while astral traveling by yourself.

If your travels seem not to have been as clear and intense as you wish, don't despair. By undergoing them in an astral meditative state, you have programmed your subconscious mind to desire the experience. Watch your dreams closely after these meditations. You may well find that your astral dreaming is carrying you where you want to go, either to intensify what you already experienced, or to supplement the experience you had.

This series of astral exercises is given to help you place markers for traveling in the astral planes and particularly through time-space. Now that you understand the basics behind such markers, you can easily find your way for other experiences.

The following descriptions will act as markers for your travels. They are offered as a variety of experiences to help you get to and from ancient Mystery celebrations and schools.

Nearly every astral traveler, sooner or later, concludes that he or she would like to participate in ancient celebrations or study in schools whose teachings have been long forgotten. Going to these places and events will provide you with personal experiences and information you can get nowhere else.

In preparation for visiting such a school, specify what kind of teacher you think would benefit you. Ask for a teacher who can help you with a specific talent or who can give you information about something you are trying to learn or understand. Don't expect a famous person. Famous people tend to be boring when actually encountered.

At one time I thought I would like to study with Socrates and Plato. These turned out to be the most boring, uninformative journeys I've ever made. Everyone there argued, picked everything apart, and never came to a conclusion on anything. They reminded me of a group of politicians.

Visits to schools eventually turn from deliberate travels to sleep-visits. You can program yourself before sleep to visit an astral school by thinking of the journey there. If you have a particular school or subject in mind, let your teachers know. Be sure to record your "dreams."

These schools may be held in a temple, a garden, an ancient building, or on some sacred site. The teacher may be any nationality, so leave your prejudices at home. You can choose a particular ancient school in a culture in which you are interested. Or you can ask to time-travel to an ancient school which will help you with your present life.

If you are doing a great deal of sleep-travel, you may find yourself getting up as tired as when you went to bed. If the schooling becomes too intense, you need to tell your teacher-guides to be less strenuous with your dream time.

Every culture had some kind of Mystery religion and/or celebrations. It is fascinating to watch the proceedings since we have little or no historical records of most of them. You will probably find that you can clearly understand part of the ritual, while other parts you either can't hear at all or come to your astral ears as a foreign language. When you are spiritually prepared, you will be able to hear all of the ceremony.

Following are several descriptions of ancient mysteries to help you in your travels. However, you can find your own markers for journeys to other celebrations by being determined and asking for help from your teacher-guides.

From the end of September to the beginning of October, the Greeks held the Greater Eleusinia in honor of Demeter, Kore, Persephone, and the holy child Iacchus. These mysteries were open to both men and women and were bound by oaths of secrecy. Eleusis means "advent," thus explaining the Divine Child in the basket of Demeter. Only the second degree initiates (the Epoptae) could participate in many of the inner rites.

Candidates for initiation marched in a torch-light procession down to the sea where they bathed in the ocean on the night before their induction into the mysteries. Then they had to fast all night in a vigil of silence. The next day they went to the great hall of Eleusis, dedicated to the goddess Demeter and her daughter.

Corn, pomegranates, and poppies were Eleusinian symbols, referring to the unseen forces that affect humans through seasonal growth and changes. As the final act of their initiation, they went veiled into the deep caverns where a single ear of wheat and other secret symbols were revealed in flashes of light.

Initiates were inducted as a group, not individually. Therefore, it seems that something happened at a psychic level which made a tremendous impression on everyone there. There seems to have been a collective spiritual vision, something so vast and wonderful that it changed lives and attitudes forever.

The most important part of these mysteries seemed to have been to take the initiates through the gates of death and back again. Participation in the Eleusinian Mysteries was said to grant life after death. Since we know that the Greeks and others knew that spirits live on after physical death, we can take this to mean that such an initiate would have conscious memories after physical death. This would enable her/him to make rational choices in reincarnation.

Although we do know a few facts about this intense spiritual experience, there are no records of exactly what went on during certain parts of these rituals.

Amazonian Dianic Worship

Anatolia or Asia Minor was one of the homes of many tribes of
Amazons. The Amazons were all-women clans ruled by sister-
queens; they conceived by visiting nearby clans with males, keeping the female babies, and sending the males to the fathers. They
did not amputate one breast, as some writers claim. The Amazons
rode horses or drove them hitched to swift war-chariots.

Their priestesses often wore vulture masks with wings. The
symbols of the New or Full Moon were worn as jewelry and during their religious rites. They were known as Moon-women, followers of the huntress goddess Artemis/Diana. Because their
goddess's symbol was the New Moon, the Amazons used the
Moon sickle in battle. Not much is reliably recorded about these
fierce tribes of women.

Their sacred worship places were in Nature settings, often
centered on or near meteorites, natural rocky monoliths, and/or
waterfalls. Their ceremonies appear to have been calculated by
the New and Full Moons, as well as the turn of the seasons.

Like many other women-only religious groups, the Amazons danced and sang themselves into an altered state of consciousness and ecstasy. They would howl at the Moon or sing out
ululating cries while they danced or ran through the dark forests.
Ancient writers told of the Amazons working themselves into
this state of Goddess-ecstasy before battles so that their wounds
did not bleed.

Since the rites of the Amazons were for women only, you
should take on the appearance of a woman (if you are male) for
participation in these mysteries.

The Secret Ceremonies of Mithras

The worship of Mithras came from the Persians. To most people,
the Sun god Mithras is known through records of the Roman soldiers, where the deity was connected with the bull sacrifice and
baptism in the animal's blood.

There were seven degrees of initiation for the mystic cele-brants. Sacred masks were worn to denote their degree: Raven (*corax*), Occult (*cryphius*), Soldier (*miles*), Lion (*leo*), Persian (*Perses*), Runner of the Sun (*heliodromus*), and Father (*pater*). These seven degrees corresponded to the seven planets known at that time.

The first three degrees were the Servants. Not much is known about the Raven initiates, but members of the Occult class were hidden behind a veil in the underground temple or cave during services. Members of the Soldier class were responsi-ble for waging war on evil under directions from the god.

When one graduated to the Lion degree, one was allowed to take part in the rituals. With the Persian degree, initiates assumed the Phrygian cap, a symbol of Mithras. Runners of the Sun and the Lion were responsible for performing much of the actual ceremonies, while the Fathers presided over all the sacred rituals. One member of the Fathers was called the Pater Patrum, meaning the Grand-Master. The Fathers were considered to be adepts in the Mithraic mysteries and held their posts until death.

Before each ceremony, all initiates took a sacred bath to wash away any sins. Members were raised to the Lion degree by a rite in which honey was placed on the tongue and hands. Upon reaching this degree, initiates could participate in the bread and wine sacrament. All members of the Mithraic religion were for-bidden to participate in overindulgences of any kind. They had to be honorable, truthful, trustworthy, and keep their vows of secrecy about the mysteries.

The baptism in the sacred *taurobolium*, probably repeated with each rise in degree, was done in remembrance of Mithras killing the great bull as ordered by the Sun. Persian myth said that from the body and blood of this bull sprang all vegetation, ani-mals, and humans. During this baptism in blood, the initiate lay in a pit below a latticed platform on which the bull was killed.

Since Mithraism was a men-only Mystery, you should take on the appearance of a man (if you are a woman) when partici-pating in these ceremonies.

Isis, the Great Goddess of Egypt

Isis was the Great Goddess of Egypt; later Her worship reached as far as Rome and Gaul. She was easily accepted because Her description could fit many Great Goddesses of different cultures.

Isis was considered to be the weaver and knotter of the threads of the *tat,* or life-plan. Her priestesses were said to control the weather by braiding or releasing their hair. Her priests, called *mesniu* (smiths), knew the special magickal arts of metalworking. It was said She gave the art of making and blowing on magick knots to Her devotees.

Because Isis was a Moon deity, her followers used the sistrum, which represented the Moon; a cat image was carved at its top. They danced, sang hymns, and played musical instruments to show Her honor. Incense, especially Kyphi, was burned while petitions for Her help were chanted.

Since Isis was also mistress of magick, Her initiates were taught powerful magickal spells. Egyptian magick was primarily of two kinds: magick to benefit the living and the dead, and magick to protect from evil and to retaliate when magickally attacked.

At the beginning of each ritual, lighted lamps were set at each of the four directions. These lamps represented the four sons of Horus, who was himself the son of Isis. Symbols were also set at these directions: East, the tat of Osiris (Isis's husband); South, a model of a palm tree; West, a figure of Anubis (the nephew who helped Isis embalm Osiris); North, a figure of a mummy, sometimes lying in a coffin. The mummy symbolized the immortality of the soul.

At the end of the ceremonies in Her temples, the ritual area was symbolically swept clean.

The Persian Fire Ceremony

Little remains of the records of the ancient sacred Persian fire ceremony. It was part of the Magis' worship of their unnamed god. Both men and women could be initiated into this group, although the requirements were stringent. All initiates had to be pure in thought, word, and deed; they did not marry, but devoted their time to studies of astrology, magick, and other pursuits.

All initiates were clothed completely in white when participating in these rituals. They also wore gauze masks that covered their noses and mouths, so that their breath would not contaminate the fire or the sacred place. Their temples stood on hills or high areas of ground away from all villages or cities. The building was quite plain: a large room with a central stone cauldron where the sacred fire was kindled and ceremonies held; and smaller rooms where members could gather for talk, prayer, and study.

The devotees of the fire ceremony gathered in their temple at dusk. The fire was ceremonially lit by the head of their group. This was followed by chants and prayers to the God of Spiritual Light. A special drink was mixed and passed among those gathered; this seems to have induced mystical visions. The head of the order would call down the god and give prophecies.

After the ritual was finished, the members gathered in the smaller rooms to talk about their visions, pray, study the stars for omens and prophecies, etc.

Ishtar of Babylon

The goddess Ishtar of the ancient Middle-Eastern cultures was known as the Queen of Heaven, Goddess of the Moon, Lady of Battles, the Shining One, Guardian of Law and Order, the Lady of Vision, and Goddess of Love.

Her symbols were the eight-pointed star, the pentagram, dove, serpents, dragons, the double serpent scepter, and the double axe. As a warrior deity, Ishtar carried a bow and rode in a chariot drawn by seven lions.

In ancient Sumeria, She had 180 shrines where women gathered daily for prayer. The night of the Full Moon, known as *Shapatu,* was the time for joyous celebrations in Her temples. At these sacred rites, called the *Qadishtu,* the women who lived as priestesses in Her shrines took lovers to express the sacredness of sexuality. Men communed with Her in these rites through sex. Once in her life every woman had to sit in the temple and wait for a man to drop a coin in her lap; the woman would have sex with this man. Unless she did this, she was not considered blessed by Ishtar and could not marry. Sexuality was said to be a gift from Ishtar. Because of this openness about sex, the later Christians called Her the Great Whore.

The temples of Ishtar were built with lush gardens around them. Everything was made as beautiful as possible to honor the goddess. Priestesses and novices sang hymns, played musical instruments, and danced in honor of their Lady. They were joyous in their celebrations, for they said that Ishtar created sex and joy in life.

Petitions were brought to the temples for every aspect of life. These were presented at the altar by the priestesses. They taught that Ishtar loved all Her children and would answer any request made from a joyful, believing heart.

Freyja, the Northern Star

Freyja was a powerful Norse goddess; She was called the Lady, the Great Goddess, and the Mistress of Cats. She owned the magickal necklace Brisingamen and kept half of the slain warriors in Her hall in Asgard. Freyja was also leader of the Valkyries, a shape-shifter, and a sage who inspired all sacred poetry. The power and knowledge of the runes were Hers before Odhinn learned them.

Wise women, seeresses, rune-mistresses, and healers were connected with Freyja, deity of magick and love affairs (not marriages). Her special female followers were called *volvas* and followed Her particular branch of magick, called *seidr*. The volvas went about the tribes giving prophecies through trance. They also did healing and occasionally laid curses. These women carried a staff with a bronze cap and wore capes, hoods, and gloves of fur.

Seidr was a feminine mystical craft, a form of magick which included soul journeying, trance, and divination. Some of its primary teachings included shape-shifting, astral body travel through the nine worlds, sex magick, and other secret techniques. These priestesses also had their own interpretation of the runes, the meanings which came before Odhinn changed them.

One of the celebrations of Freyja came at the beginning of winter; this was the *disablot*. The *disir* (goddesses) were nine women who dressed in black and carried swords. Freyja was called the great *dis*. These women went from house to house, bringing blessings to the families. If any house deserved judgment or retribution, the disir dispensed it.

Freyja was also a Moon deity. Her priestesses and followers honored Her at the Full Moon in special secret rituals.

The Rites of the Celtic Grove

The religion of the Celts involved more than the Druids. There were groups of sacred women who devoted themselves to a particular goddess. These groups often lived in sacred groves where they had temples and held schools for initiates. These groves held a special object, such as an old tree, a spring, well, or monolith which was the central focal point of the power of that place. If none of these occurred naturally, a cauldron or large bowl was set up.

Celtic priestesses sang the dying to sleep, did enchantments, prophecies, charms, birthing, and healing. They knew the power of words, stones, and herbs. For their magick, they let their hair hang loose. The priestesses laid curses for any mistreatment of women. Red-haired women were sacred to the war goddesses. The Celtic priestesses were considered important healers, judges, astronomers, teachers, oracles, and religious leaders of their clans along with the Druids.

The goddess Brigit had an exclusive female priesthood of nineteen priestesses at Kildare where they kept an ever-burning fire. These kelles were sacred prostitutes, much the same as the priestesses of Ishtar in the Middle East.

Grove rituals were held at Imbolc (February), Spring Equinox, Beltane (May), Summer Solstice, Lughnassadh (August), Autumn Equinox, Samhain (October), and Winter Solstice. They also celebrated the New and Full Moons.

After traveling to ancient schools, studying in the astral, meeting with ancient teachers, and visiting ancient Mystery celebrations, you will quite likely be offered an initiation. This may happen more than once, by different teachers in different settings. Sometimes you are warned in advance of this initiation; other times you are suddenly confronted with it. You can accept or refuse.

Be prepared to flow with whatever you see in your astral journeying to the ancient places and ceremonies. Things may happen differently from what you had in mind. On occasion you may be refused entrance. If you politely ask, an explanation will be given. Usually you are told you are not ready.

If you feel uncomfortable or simply don't like any of the places or times to which you travel, make a note of this. Then check back into your own past lives. You will discover a reason in your Akashic records. It may be due to a bad experience in another life, or it may simply be because you were denied entrance before, and never got over the rejection.

You may find yourself repeating your deliberate journey to a specific place through your astral dreams. This happens because we can absorb information more easily when the conscious mind has absolutely no participation in the process. When you have absorbed the information needed, you will move on into another class or another study experience automatically.

By making journal notes of all your astral meditations and astral dreams, you can remember more completely parts of specific ceremonies. You may even want to incorporate pieces of these ancient ceremonies into your regular Pagan rituals. This is a way to re-experience, usually at a deeper intuitive level, the sacredness and symbolism of the original ceremony. Don't try to be exact in the wording or even the ancient ceremony itself. The purpose of bringing forward remnants of these ancient rituals is to re-ignite their power which speaks directly to the human soul. The underlying purpose of all astral travel should be spiritual growth. The more we grow spiritually while within our physical bodies, the better our adjustment and advancement when we go into the astral realms to await a new birth.

Nine

The Astral Lover

One of the most controversial of astral topics is the astral lover. Most people know nothing about this, while some who do are kept from enjoying the experience by the taboos of orthodox religion.

Having a spirit lover is an experience that one must undergo in order to fully understand. I am not speaking simply of a sexual experience with just any astral entity who shows an interest. Hopefully, you wouldn't be guilty of such irresponsible action in the physical, so why succumb in the astral? The astral lover is an entity who is as loving and concerned about you as a true physical lover would be. This being loved you before you were born this time, and probably has loved you for centuries of lifetimes.

Sometimes in your long succession of lives you both existed in the physical; sometimes only one of you

113

was in the physical while the other looked on from the astral realms. But the love you felt for each other continued, even when you could meet and touch only on the astral planes. She/he is likely ready and eager to help you now, if you will acknowledge her/his existence. Like anyone who truly loves another person, this entity wants to do more than make love.

You can renew this wonderful relationship during your astral travels. This astral relationship can have all the same tenderness, warmth, and satisfaction of a physical one. Since your senses on the astral plane are more intense than on the physical, you will discover new and enhanced feelings. In this day of deadly diseases contracted through physical intercourse, astral sex is the safest sex there is, provided you don't become involved with just any spirit who shows an interest.

If you consider it logically, the physical part of sex is actually the least important part of the experience. The emotions are what put meaning and enjoyment into the sexual act. Remember, the astral body is also called the emotional body. The ability to experience all the romance, desire, excitement, and mystique of any relationship is naturally carried into the astral with you when you travel. Without these emotions, there is nothing of value in the sexual experience, physical or astral.

If all this is true, then why do orthodox religions claim that spiritual beings don't engage in "sex" and that making love with a spiritual being is sinful? The first reason they do this is that so much of the real knowledge about such relationships has been lost; they don't know the truth now, if they ever did. Second, fear makes people easier to control. Third, the orthodox religions don't want you to know anything about the astral planes. This knowledge would upset their control over people's minds and bring into question their narrow vision of an afterlife.

By now your logical mind is probably kicking around the words incubus and succubus. Nearly everyone has heard of these "nasty" entities who delight in forcing themselves sexually on sleeping people. Like the rapist and the bar-room Romeo in the physical world, these entities do exist in the astral, but they have nothing to do with the authentic astral lover. If an astral entity attempts to have sex with you while you are in your physical body, I guarantee it won't be your astral lover. It is a low-level entity who is still craving physical sex and doesn't care how she/he gets it.

This astral-bodied sexual addict is like the deceased alcoholic and the drug addict; the craving and demand are still there, and they don't care who they harm or damage in their attempts to fill that desire. Reject these entities at once. If they hook up to your root center, or the lowest chakra, they can be difficult to disconnect.

If you think one has attached itself to your root chakra, take immediate action. Begin by cleaning your aura (as described in Chapter 10), then consecrate and wear a protection amulet until you feel the danger has passed. Check your emotions and thoughts carefully and completely to determine why you attracted such an entity, if the hook-up was not by your agreement. If it was by your agreement, decide why you agreed. And don't engage in any astral lovemaking for at least six weeks. This deliberate abstinence will break any remaining connection.

Incubus is from a Latin word meaning "that which lies upon"; this is a male astral entity who preys upon women. Succubus is from the Latin word meaning "that which lies beneath"; this is a female astral entity. These words in themselves do not actually describe a low-level entity. They are merely definitions of male and female astral entities and could be used to define an astral lover. However, over the centuries, incubus and succubus have come to mean the low-level entities who come in the night to force sexual intercourse upon humans. This does not describe an astral lover, who will never force intercourse or a relationship upon a human, whether the human is in the physical or is astral traveling.

To avoid these low-level, sexually-perverted astral entities, you should insist upon a courtship period with any astral being before agreeing to engage in anything more than talk and companionship. If some strange human approached you and forcefully suggested having sex, you would be offended and probably report the person to the police. The very least you would do would be to get away from that person as fast as you could. You use the same tactics while traveling in the astral.

This brings up an important point not covered earlier. There are astral "police" who can be called upon for protection or to remove and restrain a threatening entity. These beings are easily identified by the brilliant white light which surrounds them. They will come instantly when you call. Some people mistakenly call these beings angels or guardian teachers, but they have a totally different function, type of aura, and vibration. They are police in the truest sense, and are often just as overworked. It is their responsibility to patrol the astral levels, rounding up dangerous "escaped" entities from the lower levels and returning them there.

These astral police have the power to imprison such disturbed and disturbing entities so that they cannot harass humans, either on the physical or the astral. However, some humans help these entities "break jail" by constantly thinking about them and desiring their presence. One example of this is when a lover dies in the physical and the loved one left thinks about the person constantly, wishing she/he were still available for lovemaking.

When someone dies in the physical, her/his spirit enters the astral plane with all its old prejudices, beliefs, desires, and preconceived opinions. Naturally, this carries the spirit to the precise astral plane where it will find similar companions. If that spirit can find someone in the physical with whom it still has strong ties, it can use those emotions to make contact.

I was told long ago, and have found it to be true, that the spirit of a deceased person goes to a place in the astral that corresponds to her/his personal idea of an afterlife. So-called heaven and hell are recreated in response to each spirit's expectations. If the spirit eventually progresses beyond the need to remain in that self-created heaven or hell, she/he can then move about on certain other astral planes, attending classes, learning, and preparing for reincarnation.

There are some spirits who simply reject all ideas of heaven and hell. These entities, if they are negative-minded and corrupt in their thoughts and deeds, are confined to the darkness of the lower astral levels. These lower levels are like a combination of crime-ridden ghetto slums, state penitentiary, and mental ward.

They are areas of chaos, unstable emotional energies, evil, and danger. On occasion, some of these "inmates" escape and accost astral travelers or humans in the physical.

Never assume that all spiritual entities are concerned with your good or are capable of positive deeds and thoughts. "As above, so below"—what exists here on Earth exists also on the astral planes. The low-level astral planes contain the scum of all earthly existences: the rapists, murderers, sex offenders, serial killers, thieves, incorrigible liars, etc.

The astral police also work with earth-bound spirits who haunt places, but they have no authority to forcefully remove them, unless there is an urgent call for this action. Most earth-bound haunting spirits are a nuisance, but rarely a threat to humans. If such a spirit crosses over the boundaries from minor offender to criminal, then the astral police can be asked to remove and confine the offending entity.

Be on guard against created thoughtforms sent to you by people who have sexual fantasies about you. This is a rare occurrence, but it can happen. These thoughtforms can be as aggressive as low astral entities, and they can be ejected in the same way. Immediately call for your teachers, astral lover, and the astral police to remove these thoughtforms and imprison them. Then do a protection ritual, such as described in Chapter 12, so that they can no longer invade your environment or aura.

Low-level entities and unpleasant astral experiences can also be attracted to you by present negative physical relationships. If you are involved in a relationship that degrades you or is morally wrong (such as cheating on a spouse, a spouse cheating on you and you're putting up with it, or, if single, playing around with someone else's spouse), then you can expect eventually to be faced with negative astral entities.

Keep your physical and astral morals high. You draw entities or thoughtforms to yourself through the kinds of emotional and mental states you allow to exist in your aura.

Deliberately consorting with and/or having sexual contact with low-level or negative astral entities is also certain to contaminate you with what I call psychic "lice" or psychic "venereal disease." You become like a magnet for every negative wandering thoughtform, regardless of how small. These "lice" hook into your aura and infect it. They cause a breakdown in the auric shield, opening you up to actual physical disease, emotional traumas, and a decline in everything from prosperity to good luck. Once in your aura, they will continue to grow, feeding off your auric energy until you get rid of them. Chapter 10, on healing, has suggestions for checking for these and decontaminating yourself.

The belief in sexual intercourse between humans and astral entities is very old and worldwide. However, even the ancients differentiated between the astral sexual offenders and an astral lover. These ancient peoples believed it was possible for children to be born from such relationships.

In Greek mythology, for instance, it is difficult to determine where, or if, some of the "spirits" crossed the line between willingness and force. There are many stories of Greek "gods" forcing themselves upon mortal women. Since these myths were rewritten after the take-over by the patriarchal clans, one wonders if originally the stories were of astral lovers and their human loves. Some of these "gods" who cared for their human lovers and the children produced from the relationship probably were astral lovers. Those "deities" who merely went in for rape likely were astral rapists and nothing more.

The ancient Greeks considered the offspring of these unions to be demigods. Sometimes these offspring were immediately recognized as deities or demigods and were never assumed to be in physical form, while others were said to be totally of human form and nature. Other cultures had much the same beliefs. When Christianity took over, these astral rapists and lovers were all lumped together and called demons.

The Celtic Scots knew of these astral lovers, calling them the *Leannain Sith*, or faery lovers or familiar spirits. The practice of astral sex with these entities must have been common enough, for the clergyman Robert Kirk warned against it in his book on faeries written in 1690 or 1691. Kirk says that many young men willingly cohabited with such female entities, and he calls them paramours and strumpets. Robert Kirk also writes that both men and women could have faery lovers, with the women sometimes bearing a child of the union. Geoffrey of Monmouth wrote that Merlin came from such a union of a mortal woman and a faery man. Geoffrey called these entities *daemones,* meaning "a familiar spirit." But Kirk was a Christian minister and had some very prejudiced statements to make about the practice.

In shamanic traditions and practices, this making complete contact with the Otherworlds and having sexual intercourse with a spirit entity was accepted as a common experience of the shaman. Shamans frequently speak of having astral wives or husbands with whom they have children. These children are raised in the Otherworlds by the astral parent and are never mentioned as having any physical form. The children remaining in the Otherworlds is a more common theme in cultural belief than is the one of the children being born mortal.

A few magickal traditions appear to have used the astral lover as a substitute for human sex. The remaining records list only female participants in this, but there were probably men who practiced the same procedure. Today in Mexico there are still certain female "witches" who use an unguent called *toloachi,* which they say enables them to contact their spirit lovers. This unguent contains deadly herbs, much as the flying ointment of the medieval witches. These women are said to have no need of men, something considered sinful by both the men and the churches.

This reminds one of the extorted details of the witch trials where women "confessed" to the use of certain hallucinogenic ointments. At first, the accounts of the witch's intercourse with spirit beings tell of intense pleasure. After about 1470, however, the witch-hunters decided these accounts sounded too good, so they changed them into disgusting stories.

Please don't use drugs or any "flying" concoctions to make a connection with your astral lover. Methods such as these are only likely to project you into the dangerous lower levels of the astral planes where you will have to contend with criminal types of spirits. If you don't care how you get your astral sex, then you will get just what you deserve. It won't be a pleasant experience. You will find that you opened yourself to the advances and misuse of any low-level entity that comes along. In short, you will find yourself a free prostitute for the worst kind of astral beings.

Knowing all this, you may be reluctant to search for your astral lover. Don't be apprehensive. If you keep your ethics and goals high, you will not be faced with low-level entities. Just take your time getting acquainted with your astral lover. Spend quality time expressing your innermost thoughts, feelings, and desires. Engage in a little hugging and kissing and feeling loved and cared for.

If you already have a spouse or lover, you are not in any way being unfaithful. After all, your physical companion is your lover-friend on this plane of existence, while your astral companion your lover-friend on the astral only. You will find that your astral lover will be much more tolerant of your physical relationship than the other way around. She/he knows that the physical lasts only for a set amount of time before you must make the transition to the astral planes to await a new incarnation.

It is quite natural to at first fear that you will make contact with this astral lover and feel her/his touch. Then you move on to the next stage, that of fearing that you won't make contact. Fear and tension keep you from having a positive astral experience; in fact, they will probably keep you from astral traveling at all. So try to place yourself in the position of joyfully awaiting this new experience, while at the same time not berating yourself if it doesn't happen at once.

If your spirit lover tells you that you were someone famous in a past life, consider it a compliment but not fact. Lovers often say such things to each other, but don't expect them to be taken literally. Such a statement isn't meant to be a lie, only an expression of love.

A true astral lover will not be jealous of your physical relationships, your present spouse or lover. A true spirit lover will not want you to be alone during this physical existence. She/he will rejoice when you are happy, and console you when you are depressed and sad. This being will help you in any way possible to improve your life, your health, and your spiritual enlightenment, all without demanding anything in return. Your spirit lover will always work for your benefit and give you good advice. She/he can also warn you of upcoming problems and help heal you when you are ill. The astral lover can provide you with information you need, aid you in astral travel itself, and guide you in seeing and taking advantage of opportunities to better your life. As with all lovers, you will probably want to do something nice in return at some time or another. An astral lover might suggest a repayment in the form of working to heal or help another person, physical or astral. Use your common sense when considering such a suggestion. If the astral lover is truly working for your benefit, she/he will never suggest anything that is wrong or against your morals.

Don't be afraid to ask your astral lover for help. If you need help with a problem or wish to improve your life (materially or otherwise), discuss this with your lover. Like anyone in love, this being will help all she/he can. In return, don't talk about your astral love life, thus exposing your lover to hate and ridicule. This may mean not telling your physical lover or spouse about your astral relationship, especially if you have a mate who would not understand. After all, you really aren't "cheating." Why create unnecessary trouble when the second relationship is actually a spiritual relationship?

Be realistic about your astral lovemaking. Don't lose yourself to loving on the astral plane exclusive of physical relationships. Such an attitude and behavior will create an imbalance in your aura and cause problems.

By now you should be comfortable with your astral traveling and experiencing things with your psychic senses. But perhaps the idea of an astral relationship, including sex, still strikes you as impossible. Think carefully about your past astral experiences for a moment. Didn't you feel the touch of your teacher-guide? Couldn't you feel all emotions when you reviewed a past life? Don't block yourself from this new experience because you might be frightened or turned off by the term "sex." Some physical relationships endure without any sexual connotations; if this is your wish, you can also keep your astral loving at this level. You never have to jump into sex with anyone, either here or out there. Set your parameters and go at your own speed.

Remember, the human-made concepts of time and space are not the same in the astral as we perceive them to be in the physical. Dr. John Mariani, a member of the New York Academy of Sciences, made some startling discoveries concerning Albert Einstein's theories about time and space. Under certain conditions, time does not respond in what we consider to be the usual manner. Space and time can interchange with each other rather suddenly. Looking at this idea from a spiritual standpoint, if the vibrations of an individual are of a certain higher frequency than normal, such as happens during astral travel, that individual can make full contact with astral entities.

In seeking and being with an astral lover, you must take greater care in how you exit from your physical body than usual. You certainly don't want to attract the attention of any low-level entities. In previous chapters, I spoke about leaving through the higher chakras or light centers. The chakra through which you exit for your astral journey should be carefully considered. Avoid the first two lower chakras. Leaving through them is a sure ticket to the lower astral levels, places you want to avoid. The solar plexus center will tie you into pure emotions. By using this light center you may open up communication with deceased spirits who once had an emotional bond with you in some way. This may or may not be pleasant.

You really want a higher center so you can make a more spiritual connection. After all, this relationship should be a highly spiritual experience, even if you do eventually become involved in an astral sexual relationship. Use the brow or crown centers as exit-points when visiting your astral lover. By doing this, you avoid attracting low-level entities and won't end up somewhere on the lower astral plane fighting off perverts.

Before embarking on your astral journey, tune your thoughts to those of love, companionship, and a true lover. Prepare yourself by wearing cologne or perfume, brushing your hair, all the usual preparations for a date. You might even arrange your altar or a table in your ritual area with a pink candle and some flowers. Wear a sexy nightgown or nice pair of pajamas or even remain nude when you go to bed. If this arouses your physical lover, enjoy the experience. Your astral lover won't be jealous. In fact, the physical loving will make it easier for you to open your emotions and psychic senses to your astral lover.

Go out onto the astral as you usually do. Be sure that you pull your consciousness up to at least the brow center before exiting. Once in the astral, send out your call for your astral lover. You will probably be surprised to find your lover waiting for you. Connections from past lives will have made such a strong bond between the two of you that an instant's thought will bring you together.

Upon meeting, and being aware of this being for the first time, you need to spend a few minutes looking at her/him. Notice the color of the hair and eyes, the contours of the face, and what nationality the being has chosen to represent. At the first remembered meeting, the astral lover will assume the features and clothing of a past life that meant a lot to both of you. In this way, she/he will help you to recall subconsciously memories from that period of time.

Feel the loving touch as you clasp hands with your lover. Ask for a name. You may even lovingly embrace in a hug that will fill you with intense joy. Your lover may suggest that the two of you go to the garden temple where the Akashic records are kept. I assure you this will be an enlightening experience. If you had difficulty reading and/or understanding your Akashic records before, this is a perfect opportunity to see them in a better light. After all, you will have with you the best interpreter and guide you could want. Your lover will choose those lifetimes, of course, which involved the two of you, but at later times she/he will willingly help you to see and understand any other lifetimes you wish to see.

Spend several astral journeys getting to know this lover. She/he may take you to interesting places for visits: in the astral planes themselves, to present-day locations, or forward and backward through time itself. If you have had difficulty contacting the spirit of a deceased person, the astral lover will do everything possible to arrange for this to happen. Not only that, the lover will be a guardian for the entire time you are out on the astral.

Eventually there will come a time when you wish to express your joy and love in other ways than just an embrace or a warm kiss. Don't expect astral sex to be like physical sex; it isn't. Your astral lover will be gentle, guiding you into the astral experience with great love. I can only give you the basics of what to expect; there is no way possible to express the intensity and beauty of the experience.

When you face your spirit lover for this occasion, you will feel your throat center begin to increase in size. Allow this to happen as it helps to clear all the chakras by removing obstructions. This expansion also increases your creativity and intensifies your psychic talents. Even without all these side benefits, this enlarged throat center produces an almost sexual tingling throughout your astral body.

Then you and your lover move together, face to face. When both your lines of chakras are lined up, a form of light center intercourse begins. The exchange of energy is fantastic. This type of spiritual intercourse makes physical sex seem like a child's game. You have to experience it to understand fully what I mean.

Occasionally, this astral intercourse will produce a corresponding reaction in the physical body and you will experience an orgasm. Or you may awake in a very sexy mood and surprise your physical mate with an unexpected invitation to lovemaking.

Loving on the astral planes with an astral being in this manner is not evil, sinful, or dirty. It is a bona fide spiritual experience, one that orthodox religions don't want you to know about. Knowing the truth behind this ancient secret makes it possible for a single, widowed, or divorced person to live a sexually satisfied, spiritual, and happy life without the marriage bonds demanded by the churches. This knowledge puts you outside the control of such organizations and other interfering people. It also makes you resistant to clumsy proposals of unwanted and insincere suitors and the undesired attempts of matchmakers. You are your own independent person.

Another side benefit of having an astral lover is that she/he doesn't want you to live alone if you truly desire to have a physical companion. In fact, the astral lover will help to bring a compatible companion to you. Your relationship with your astral lover will prepare you mentally and emotionally for the time when this "right" person comes into your physical life. You will have learned how to give of yourself and what to expect in return. This astral preparation will eliminate any compromises that often occur in physical relationships, such as one person giving everything and the other only taking.

If you are in a physical relationship that is or has turned undesirable, your astral lover will help you disengage in a peaceful manner, protecting you if necessary. Your astral lover will remain with you, teaching you on the astral how to recover your self-respect and dignity. Then when you are ready for a compatible physical relationship once more, the astral lover will aid you by bringing the proper person into your environment.

You may also choose to experience astral sex if you and your physical lover or spouse are separated by distance and want to continue your sexual relationship. Make plans to meet on the astral planes on a particular night. Make all your preparations, as you would for meeting your astral lover. Hold your loved one's face in your mind as you drift off to sleep. Exit through the brow or crown centers. The two of you will meet on the astral, sharing much the same experience you did with your astral lover.

A word of caution here: don't arrange this astral meeting unless your physical lover is in complete agreement. That would be tantamount to rape. You certainly wouldn't want other astral travelers to force themselves on you without your permission, or be invading your astral-dream time with suggestions you don't want and are not interested in. If your physical lover isn't open to the suggestion of meeting on the astral for a sexual experience, don't push the point. In fact, if your partner is dead set against the idea of the astral at all, don't even mention it. Instead, spend your time with your astral lover, who will always be happy to see you.

Acknowledging your personal astral lover and choosing to spend time with her/him can definitely help with your development and progress, both in astral travel and spiritual growth. With your lover's help, you can improve your material life, get better results with your astral magick and healings, and have a

125

better warning system against psychic attacks or upcoming negative physical events. The astral lover can be friend, advisor, teacher, protector, and lover all rolled into one. You need never feel alone and despondent again. Your own special lover-friend is only a thought away.

The beauty of this special relationship is that it has endured for centuries and will keep on enduring for centuries more. Your lover was there with you as you waited to experience your birth into this world, and she/he will be waiting when you leave it once more to return to the spirit realms.

Ten

Healing
in the
Astral

The last chapters of this book deal with more advanced uses of astral travel. Before projecting out into the astral realms to perform a healing, however, you should take the time to understand thoroughly some of the things which affect the results of healings and which may differ from your healing work on the physical plane.

Practice the astral healing techniques described until you feel confident enough to experiment with procedures you are shown by your teachers or discover for yourself. No one's personal healing methods are carved in stone. What works best for one healer in the astral may not be the right technique for another.

The average person can change her/his brainwave patterns to produce up to 80 percent Alpha waves simply by closing her/his eyes. So making the transition to an altered state of consciousness isn't really that difficult. However, beware of those individuals who can sit down with a bio-feedback machine and produce nearly 100 percent Alpha waves without really trying. To the majority of these people it is merely a game; they would have no self-discipline to work in the astral planes. Unless they would get some personal gratification out of astral travel, they couldn't be bothered. So don't judge yourself by their performances with bio-feedback.

The average person uses only 10 percent of her/his potential ability because we operate mostly in the Beta mode during our everyday activities. To reach the other 90 percent, that power which produces healings and manifestations, we need to get into the subconscious mind by means of the Alpha waves.

Once we can visualize something and accept that it is true, our nervous system (or that of the person we are trying to heal) will accept it as true. Those nerve ends which have been dissociated will come together to form a coordinated juncture of the dendrites and axones in the brain. This creates a better flow of auric electrical energy needed for healing. It may take several visualizations and acceptances before this happens.

Most people don't have their desires manifested because they keep changing their minds about the end result. Their thoughts are a confusion of constantly changing ideas, with no concrete, determined goals in mind. These are the types of people who simply can't make a decision on much of anything. They are afraid they might make the wrong decision, so they make none. They are afraid they might not like their goals if they should happen, so they subconsciously undermine their efforts to reach those goals.

This applies to both the healer and the person to be healed. There must be a united agreement that a healing will take place. How that healing occurs can remain open to individual interpretation, but that fact that a healing is desired must be a unanimous decision. If there is the slightest hesitation on this by either the healer or the ill person, the healing will not happen or will be a struggle every inch of the way.

Astral Work I

Before beginning your healing work, you need to go out onto the astral planes, create a healing "office" for yourself, and learn everything you can from qualified teachers there.

There are a number of healing centers on the astral planes to which you can travel astrally to learn healing. The Celts speak of the Fortunate Isle which is ruled by a priestess or goddess; this entity, with her sisters, can teach not only the powers of astral flight and shape-shifting, but various healing therapies. The ancient Egyptians called upon the goddesses Isis and Maat. Shamans travel to the Upperworld and/or the Underworld where they have established healing places; there they communicate with their animal helpers. The Greeks visited earthly temples of Asclepias and Hygeia; these physical healing centers were counterparts of astral ones. Nearly every ancient civilization spoke of the unseen healing temples.

Astral experiences are not daydreams; they are valuable experiences in heightened consciousness and altered states of consciousness, which reach directly to and influence the subconscious mind.

It is necessary to be in a positive mood when attempting astral travel. If you are angry or full of resentment, you are very likely to find yourself among low-level negative entities or in some nightmare experience. To avoid this, check your mood and then plan exactly where you want to go in the astral before you leave the physical body.

The choice of chakra through which you exit into the astral has a direct bearing on the kind of experience you will have. Avoid using the two lower light centers! The solar plexus center can be used for staying close to the earth levels, such as in checking on someone. However, I would suggest avoiding it for healing purposes since this center is entirely emotional.

When you first make trips into the astral to visit the healing centers, it is natural to be afraid to touch a spiritual being. This may keep you from successful astral travel, or throw you back into the physical if you do get out. Later, the problem turns into the stress of worrying about not touching such a being, which can have the same effect.

When astral traveling to Otherworld healing centers, you are likely to hear ethereal music and see flashing colored lights. Certain types of music and colors have been widely used in healing for centuries.

Sometimes it is necessary to view a person's Akashic records in order to determine the true cause of an illness. Some physical and mental problems originate in past lives. They made such an emotional impact at the time that they became engraved on the soul pattern; strong negative emotions ride along with us from lifetime to lifetime until we acknowledge and rid ourselves of them.

Tell a person (only if she/he is open to the concept) about the past life event which probably triggered the illness. However, you must keep in mind that if the person isn't willing or prepared to overcome karma, telling her/him will do no good. The person has to be willing to help her/himself by no longer accepting the situation and by doing everything possible, including magick, to overcome it.

Healers often run up against sick people who begin syphoning off the healer's energy as soon as the connection is made. This leaves the healer in a depleted state, open to negative thought-forms and astral intrusions. A healer cannot be effective if she/he has to guard against such vampirism, since an astral connection needs to be made for the healing to work. Decide if the "patient" is just out for free energy, or if the person is subconsciously so low in vital energy that she/he is desperate. Act accordingly.

One method for a slight increase in your own energy is to hold the tips of your fingers against the ends of the needles of pines or cedars. Deep rhythmic breathing and regular meditation are also energizing.

Healing yourself is much more difficult than healing someone else. Healers should run a regular check on their auras and light centers, looking for the tiniest erosions of their energy flow. Preventative maintenance is better than finding a full-blown problem.

Sooner or later you will run up against another healer who will subtly begin pumping you about your patients and your successes. *Never* talk about your patients and their problems! You should consider yourself under the same ethical code as doctors:

privileged communication. Even if you should talk about your patients, you will discover that such a healer will likely send you a wave of intense jealousy. To this type of person, healing has become a kind of sport where only the scores matter. Avoid these people if at all possible.

Before going out into the astral as usual, arrange for your teacher-guides to meet you. As soon as you are out onto the astral planes, these teachers will guide you to the section where the healing temples lie. There are a number of these centers, so follow your instincts in choosing the one that appeals to you. My own personal choice is an onion-domed building of white marble that sits high on a hill.

Although each temple will have a different inner layout, they will be similar in their content. There will be a large worship area, a section where classes are given, libraries, and a number of smaller rooms available to practicing healers. You may want to have your teacher-guides give you a tour, introducing you to the astral healers and teachers there, before deciding upon your working area.

When you first enter your astral "office," it will be a bare room. The first step of your astral training will be to decorate this room through visualization. Take your time deciding what you want, where you want it, and bringing it into astral reality.

Begin by furnishing this space with a large, comfortable table, waist-high. Provide a pillow, blanket, and wide steps for the patient to use. Beside it place a chair for those who feel uncomfortable lying down. Situate some type of overhead lighting above the table so you can easily see your patient. At least one wall should be bare and a bright white color. By placing the patient in front of this wall, you can see the aura plainly. Have a narrow table nearby to hold whichever astral healing instruments you need. A full-length mirror or one wall of mirrors is also useful.

You can add windows onto a pleasant view or have no windows at all. The walls can be left plain or hung with pictures and posters. This "office" is entirely yours to decorate as you wish. Design and decorate in any way that makes you comfortable when you are there.

131

Before you call the astral forms of any patients to your healing space, you need to visit it alone several times until you are familiar and comfortable with it. Take as many astral journeys as necessary to create this space to your satisfaction.

Provide yourself with a spiral-bound or loose-leaf notebook to use as a journal for all your astral work. Write in it each time you finish with a deliberate astral journey. This will help you gauge your progression.

The Aura

The aura which surrounds a person will be the first point of contact for diagnosing problems. On the physical plane, some people can see auras, others cannot. Nearly every healer runs her/his hands around and/or through an aura to detect abnormalities, such as flares, unusually hot or cold sections, or breaks in the auric shield. Almost everyone in metaphysics and magickal endeavors has their own way of defining an aura.

Each being and object is surrounded by an individualized cocoon of astral energy called an aura. Humans have auras which are more individualized than those of animals, animals more than inanimate objects. There are exceptions to this, however. Some animals have evolved so far that they have a distinct, knowing, almost human personality. The auras of these special animals will be as individualized as those of any human.

An inanimate object which has been the center of concentrated focus for years or centuries will also have an individualized aura. One finds this in ancient sacred stones, worship areas, and religious objects. This aura can be particularly strong if the stone, area, or statue has been situated over an Earth-power line. You can determine this by simply walking into such a place or being near such a stone or object. Your skin will begin to prickle; the hair on your arms will stand up; you may even get the distinct feeling you are being watched.

The aura, being composed of astral energy and/or various forms of astral energy, can be molded into a different texture by the astral healer, even though this energy has become individualized around a particular person, animal, or object. This is because of the "cellular" make-up of this energy. Astral energy in and of itself contains vast power but has no individualization. Even when individualized, auric energy has a certain degree of flexibility. A healer working on the astral planes can remold this energy in an aura to reflect a more positive form, thus creating a healing. This composition of astral energy is also why any trained magician can draw on this energy and use it to form an astral creation of any kind which can then manifest in the physical.

Spiritual astral energy is everywhere; it exists in an inexhaustible supply, ready for whatever use the adept makes of it. This energy is what healers use to repair the aura, fill it with vitality, and create the healing. Magicians use it to create thoughtforms that will draw to them prosperity, opportunity, and love.

The aura of each person's astral energy is composed of layers of different intensities of energy. The density increases closer to the body. For most people, the strongest part of their aura extends only five to six inches from the physical body. From that point, it rapidly fades in intensity until it can no longer be detected.

The subconscious mind attracts this astral energy to make the aura. It uses the aura as a reservoir of healing and creating power. Through contact with the mind, the aura becomes a mirror of the physical, mental, emotional, and spiritual health of the individual. The subconscious mind also uses the aura as a warning device to signal to the psychic senses of danger. The aura shows indications of a disease long before it is manifested in the physical body itself.

Scientists have conducted tests on the effect of such methods as prayer and psychic healing when the healer is in one place and the recipient (human, animal, or plant) is up to 3,000 miles away. Distance proved no barrier to the healing process. The best results came from those healers who knew how to go into an altered state of consciousness (the astral plane). Therefore, astral travel for the purpose of healing and magick is important and can be more effective than astral-dream healing or physically working on the patient's aura.

Since this auric energy is made up of creating astral energy, our positive and negative thoughts build disease or good health, some of our good and bad luck, etc., right in our aura out of this astral energy. Negative conditions ferment there until their effect impacts upon the physical body and also blows outward, creating a flare or damaged area in the aura. Positive conditions also grow there but don't cause aura or body damage. Both of these conditions act as magnets, drawing to the aura other similar energies.

The aura, or auric shield, around the human body is a rough oval in shape. If you notice bulges or flares, this is an indication of illness. Bulges and flares usually are an indication of fermenting auric conditions caused from within, or by the diseased or troubled person.

Conditions of the Aura

The aura can be full, flaring, tight to the body, containing holes, bands of color, dark areas, and areas of heat and/or cold. An aura which extends at least five to six inches or more from the physical body shows a healthy life in all areas. If the entire aura is tight to the body (one to two inches), the person is withdrawing from life. One often sees this in dying people. You will also find this closed, tight aura in people who don't want you reading them.

Holes in the aura have already been mentioned; they are damaged areas, generally caused from the outside. Dark patches should be considered in connection with the areas of the body they are near. These can be the beginning of auric tears or an indication of a coming disease in that bodily section. Flares or spikes coming out of the aura are a sign of distress from within. The person is probably undergoing emotional and/or mental distress of which you may not be aware. In time, the person will damage her/his own aura when these flares break through the auric shield.

Areas of heat and/or cold can indicate the place of an existing physical disease. Some healers feel heat with their hands when brushing the aura over these areas, while others will feel cold. With a little practice, you will discover for yourself which you feel. Bands of color can be read in several ways. If these bands match the chakra colors in the correct positions, you are merely seeing fully working light centers pulsing through the aura. If the colors are pure and clear, but don't match the chakras, you need to determine the meaning by the width of the band (which will tell you how intense the person feels about something) and where it is located in conjunction to the body (which will help you determine how that color meaning will affect the patient's life).

Everyone, at one time or another, gets wounds or tears in her/his aura. These are sometimes called "etheric leakage." Tears in an aura allow energy and vitality to be lost, causing the person to feel tired. These tears also allow in pre-disease states of mind. These wounds and tears can be caused by attack from the outside. The person with the damaged aura may have at one time been over-tired, depressed, or dealing with a difficult situation. If this person then came in contact with a person who had a strong negative aura and wished her/him harm in some way, the person's aura would be bombarded by negative thoughtforms. These thoughtforms burrowed into the weakened aura like termites, creating holes through which even more energy was lost.

The person doing the damage need not be a magician casting spells. Ancient peoples knew what ill-wishing meant. Strong thoughts have power to become entities in the astral. A strong, positive, undamaged aura also acts as a shield from influences and/or contamination from other auras. Ancient initiates knew this and worked daily to keep their auras strong. They also learned to heed auric warning signals. They learned to read the auras of others for healing, truth, intentions, and for prophecies. They could tell which people had attracted low-level entities themselves, and which had had such beings attached to them by the ill-wishing of others.

When two auras are in close proximity, there will be an automatic struggle for domination, even though the two people are not consciously aware of this. Usually one aura will tend to predominate. Other people will try intentionally to dominate and control by sending threads of their aura to attach to yours. Manipulators and intimidators have fine-tuned this action, at least on a subconscious level. If you have to be around people you recognize as having this negative controlling attitude, keep your guard up at all times.

Psychic vampires are those who, consciously or subconsciously, are willing to feed off the auric energy of others. You probably are already well acquainted with some of these people. You are feeling wonderful, positive, and full of energy. A "friend" drops by, "because I always feel so much better when I see you." The person's entire conversation is negative, full of the person's current aches and pains, how terrible she/he is treated by others, and on and on. You know the type. As the visit wears on, you become tired and depressed, while this "friend" seems to get more energetic by the moment. By the time the person finally leaves, you are ready to take two aspirin and crawl into a corner.

This is a psychic vampire. Believe me, if you are unfortunate enough to have this kind of person for a friend, you don't need any enemies. These people can be very subtle and are determined to keep the friendship going. They will tear down your morale with criticism in one sentence, while giving you a half compliment with the next. Worse yet, they are tearing holes in your aura, attaching feeder threads from their aura to yours, and draining you dry! If they couldn't feed off the auric energies of others (and these types will have a number of "friends" they visit), they couldn't exist long in the physical. Their own auras are so faulty they waste energy. But they find it too demanding to create more for themselves from the cosmic source; that would require self-responsibility. They would rather feed off others. Avoid them if at all possible.

Keeping negative and/or wrong company will attract psychic "lice" or "vermin" to your aura. These negative thought-forms grow like ticks, gaining strength off the energy they suck up. They exist as both large and small thoughtforms which will also attach to your aura when it is weakened by strong negative emotions. They can eventually change the energy in your aura to match their negative level of being. If not cleaned out and destroyed, they act like a cancer. Psychic vermin can also be picked up through association with negative or "bad" astral entities. These "lice" will multiply if left unchecked.

Astral Work II

I have placed the color explanations of the aura after this astral work so you won't be influenced the first time you look at your own aura in the astral. After you return from this astral journey, make careful notes about everything you saw in your aura. This will give you clues to what you need to correct.

Before beginning your actual healing work on others, you need to take a good look at your own aura. Go to your astral healing temple. Before going to your individual space, you might want to spend a few moments in the worship area preparing yourself spiritually.

Enter your healing space and stand before the mirror. Order your lighting to go from bright to dim. This helps in correctly seeing the aura in the mirror. If you are having difficulty seeing your aura, try half-closing your eyes while you look into the mirror.

Look at an area about four to five inches from your bodily form. Colors and symbols will begin to appear around your reflection. Carefully note these and their position relative to various parts of your body. Can you connect any abnormalities with present physical problems or discomforts?

When you are finished with this examination, you can return to your physical body. If you feel that any problems might be connected with past lives, you might consider making a trip to the Akashic records center. Until you are experienced at checking these records, call upon your teacher-guides for help. Carefully note whether these problems are connected with past life relationships and/or events, or whether they have their origin strictly in the present life.

When you return to your physical body, write down everything you saw and learned in a journal. This physical activity will impress upon your subconscious mind the need to remember and learn from your astral healing travels. Take whatever steps you feel are necessary to correct any upcoming problems revealed by your check of your aura.

Aura Colors

Reading the aura's colors will help you determine what mental, physical, emotional, and spiritual state the person is in. The colors of the aura are developed through the molding of the astral energy to a specific purpose. These auric colors can show you what is already present, even though the sick person doesn't give you the correct information. These colors will also indicate a problem prior to its physical manifestation.

Astral entities also have auras, which can be read by the colors and symbols within those auras, just as with a physical person's aura. Since astral entities do not have illnesses as we know them, checking an astral aura will help you decide what true motives such a being has. Their auras will, however, reflect their mental, emotional, and spiritual states.

Prominent colors in auras are pink, red, orange, yellow, blue, green, indigo, purple, white, gold, silver, gray, black, and brown. There are also varying shades of these colors. Color meanings are determined by whether the shade is pure, light, dark, or swirled with another color.

Pink can mean true love, friendship, and the natural innocence found in children. Dark pink means the love or friendship is developing toward possessiveness. A lighter shade is timidity.

Pure red can mean lots of vitality and activity. Dark red is anger, resentment, lust, and exploding temper. Light red is connected with waning energy levels.

Clear orange symbolizes a feeling of personal power and the strength to change personal events to your satisfaction. Dark orange is seen when someone is on a power trip. Pale orange represents a feeling of either personal control slipping from your grasp or not making an effort for personal control of the life.

A bright, sunny yellow is often seen in the auras of creative and intellectual people; it shows the working power of the mind. A dark yellow represents sudden changes which are not to the individual's liking. A pale, almost washed-out yellow can be found in the auras of those who have lost interest in learning anything new.

True healers carry a lot of pure blue in their auras; this blue represents harmony and an understanding of other creatures. It can also mean upcoming journeys or transitional periods that will go smoothly. Very pale blues can symbolize a person who is just learning about healing or one who is beginning to give up that talent. Dark blues are associated with disharmony in life.

Green is a Nature color, one associated with fertility of the mind, body, and spirit. People who work with their hands, as well as gardeners and Nature lovers, will show this color strongly. Pale green can mean a new beginning in life, while a green so dark as to be almost black will often indicate a problem in relationships or marriage.

Indigo or turquoise is associated with one who is able to access her/his Akashic records and put to good use the knowledge found there. It is also found in the auras of those who spend quality time astral traveling. If this is a very dark color, it represents karmic problems that are not being faced. Pale indigo symbolizes a beginning of awareness of the importance of karma and the Akashic records.

Purple is a powerful color. A true shade of this color represents psychic and spiritual growth, while a dark shade shows a tendency toward misuse of these talents and a craving for the power gained through their use. Violet, a pale shade of purple, indicates one who is balancing out her/his karma and intent upon replacing undesirable habits.

White shows spiritual guidance and will often indicate the presence of personal teachers and guides. The person with a brilliant white in her/his aura is being directed into the right paths for growth and learning to see beyond illusions. This person is centered and calm. There are no dark or light shades of white.

Gold is the color of success in one or more areas of the life. Dark gold shows greed, while a pale, beautiful gold indicates a growing awareness of the person's right to be successful.

Silver is an occult color, one that symbolizes gaining and developing psychic talents. It will also appear in the auras of people who are especially dedicated to the Goddess. Silver often appears in small quantities when astral teachers are healing and soothing the emotions of their charge. For dark silver, see gray.

Gray is an ambivalent color. It symbolizes depression, a loss of confidence, a negative turn of mind. Lighter shades indicate the approach or beginning of these problems, while dark shades show up when these problems are severe. People who have dark gray spots in their auras are developing diseases.

Black is also an ambivalent color. It must be read according to the other colors and symbols in the aura. Black can mean deep pessimism and feeling bound or unable to do anything about a negative situation. On the other side, black represents a person who is working to repel psychic attack and defend her/himself against dark magick. When such a person is reversing the effects of negative spells and thoughtforms, changing her/his power into positive energy, the black in this person's aura will be shot with silver sparkles.

Brown is an Earth color, one associated with elementals, faeries, elves, and other such entities. One who has brown in any shade in her/his aura will have close connections with these entities as well as with the animal kingdom.

Astral colors, including those seen in the seven light centers, are especially vivid. Sometimes these colors seem to be a blend of two colors without being mixed. A color can seem both red and yellow without being orange.

Astral Healing III

Before beginning an actual healing process, you need to gain more experience with seeing auras, particularly while you are in your astral healing center. A good way to do this is to check the auras of your teacher-guides, friends, family, pets, and even your home. Ask the cooperation of the humans, astral beings, and animals involved, and then let them appear against the blank white wall or facing the mirror of your "office." You might want to view them against both the wall and the mirror so you can determine which works best for you.

Your teacher-guides will ordinarily have very bright, clear colors surrounding them. There will also be symbols in their auras, denoting their primary interests.

The humans and animals may well have trouble spots in their auras. Note any dark or muddy colors, flares, or ruptures in the auric shield.

Viewing the aura of your home is something seldom considered by healers. However, since auras are around inanimate objects and can influence you through interaction of their aura and yours, you need to keep an eye on them. The aura around your home is a kind of early-warning system for incoming negativity, or negativity that is taking root without your knowledge.

Make notes in your journal upon your return. If you discovered problems in your home's aura, consider whether it is caused from within or without, and take action.

Symbols in the Aura

Symbols commonly seen in auras are spots, a Moon sickle, Sun, stars, hearts, flowers, chalice, dagger, watery ripples, animals and birds, lightning, weapons, and occupational symbols.

Spots depend upon their color; they usually represent areas in the aura that are in the process of being torn or wounded. Shifting dark blotches, which remind one of amoeba as they move through the aura, are signs of psychic "lice" or contamination.

Hearts represent love and affection; flowers are seen with generous and giving people. When a person is vacillating and can't, or won't, make a decision on something, her/his aura often has a rippling look to it, like looking through gently moving water. Occupational symbols (pens, artist's materials, hammers, cooking utensils, etc.) are clues to both the regular job this person holds and her/his hobbies.

Animals and birds can be symbolic of pets this person has or would like to have. These creatures can also represent shamanic helpers in the astral planes.

Lightning will appear either when a person is about to explode in temper or when something dramatic is about to occur in that person's life. Daggers can be seen in auras when a person would like revenge for something that has happened. This symbol can also occur when someone is under psychic attack. A weapon symbol can mean attack, wanting revenge, or an occupation (such as a police officer or military person). Some weapon symbols are deliberately or subconsciously placed there for protection.

You are likely to see the Moon sickle in the aura of a Goddess follower or a person who subconsciously is affected by the Moon's phases. The Moon can also represent a spiritual awakening, especially through magick. The stars are spiritual symbols; there may be one star for each spiritual and astral teacher and advisor connected with that person. The Sun can be seen in the auras of those who have experienced or are about to experience a change in their lives for the better.

People who have undergone a meaningful spiritual initiation in either the physical or astral will often have a chalice, the

Moon, stars, and the Sun showing plainly in their auras. The chalice or goblet symbolizes dramatic experiences about to occur which will change the person's life drastically, depending upon how she/he reacts to the experience.

Astral Healing IV

Working on aura repair in the astral will be one of your first tasks in your healing space. Have a patient in mind who would not mind your examining and helping her/him.

Before calling the patient to your astral "office," enter it alone. Decide which instruments you might find useful: a healing wand with a crystal tip; a laser-cleaner; a vacuum to suck up impurities; a soft brush; a pitcher to hold liquid light; a pair of long tweezers for removing objects; rolls of astral repair tape; cans of astral putty for repairs; a large basin for discarded debris. You can create any astral tool you want. If you miss something and discover later that you need it, simply create it. All these tools should go on the narrow table next to the examination table.

Mentally call your patient to your healing space. Have the person first stand before the white wall or mirror so you can look over her/his aura. When you have noted any problems, have the patient lie down on your examination table.

Begin by running your hands around the aura to detect any weaknesses in it you might have missed in observation. These will be apparent by areas of heat or cold. Using your laser-cleaner and vacuum, dislodge and discard any impurities you find. If they won't come loose in this way, you might have to use the tweezers and carefully remove each one. Throw everything into the basin to be destroyed.

Using pieces of the astral tape or globs of the putty, repair any tears in the aura. If you worked directly on a bodily organ or part, repair that also. Brush away any excess when you are finished. Now, using your hands or the healing wand, go over the entire aura, smoothing it as much as you can.

If you found flares coming from within, try to suck up the excess energy before smoothing the aura. These flares, however, will return unless the patient takes personal action to remove the emotional problem coming from within.

Pour the patient a glass of liquid light to drink before she/he leaves. This will help in calming the patient's emotions and balancing her/his aura. When you return from your journey, write your experiences in your journal.

The Seven Major Light Centers

Every human has seven major energy transformers in her/his astral body. These are direct pipelines to the cosmic or astral energy of the universe. In the Sanskrit, these transformers were known as chakras, or wheels of light. When viewed by the psychic senses, these centers appear as rapidly rotating wheels of different colored lights. These are lined one above the other, reaching from the base of the spine to the top of the head.

The seven chakras or light centers found in the astral body are of vital importance in determining whether a person is balanced or unbalanced, well or sick. The light centers should all be of a pure, clear color for the psychic energy to be flowing properly. A dull or diminished color in one or more of these centers is an indication of problems.

The normal, natural colors of these light centers are root center, red; spleen, orange; solar plexus, yellow; heart, green; throat, silvery blue; brow, indigo; crown, violet to white.

The most active of the chakras in the average person are the three lower ones: the solar plexus (the emotional center), the root center (connected with the sexual organs), and the spleen center (seat of mental attitudes).

Right in the navel area of your abdomen is the seat of the solar plexus chakra. Ancient cultures often called this area the "second brain" or "lower mind" because it contains bundles of vital nerves which join other nerve bundles near the heart center.

The lower two light centers draw much of their energy from the earth's auric field. The root center has long been called the dwelling place of the Kundalini by the Hindu people.

Sometimes when you try to "turn" these wheels, you will find them turning backward from your efforts. This turning backward during healing is often caused by the fact that you are facing the patient, and sunwise to you is backward to them.

A person involved in low sexual activities, addiction to alcohol or drugs, compulsive overeating, or refusal to accept responsibility for her/his behavior has a blockage in the root center.

All blockage will be apparent in the small size and muddy or dark coloring of a light center. It is not unusual for someone who has experienced a traumatic childhood loss to find blockages in the first three light centers. The blockage may even reach as far as the heart chakra.

Since the spleen center is the first of the centers not getting most of its energy directly from Earth vibrations, it is usually the first to be affected by psychic impressions and development. On the psychic level, this center awakens a sensitivity to all kinds of astral influences. Discernment of spirits must be practiced as this center begins to work more freely. If you are balanced, this presents no problem. If you need work on self-discipline and control, then you will have to use extra awareness when dealing with any astral entity.

The solar plexus center is strongly influenced by emotions. It is the center of empathy and identification, especially with other people. If you think you are not affected by the projection of the emotions of others, just watch what you subconsciously do the next time you are in an unpleasant situation: you will automatically cross your arms directly over this center!

Astral Work V

Mending a patient's aura will not be quite as effective unless you also try to correct any imbalances and color disturbances in the seven light centers.

Call the patient into your astral healing space. After working on her/his aura, have the patient stand against the blank white wall. Look carefully at each of her/his light centers, beginning at the root center and ending with the crown of the head. Are any of the light centers off-color and small? Run your hands over these centers. Is the intake of energy into any of these centers restricted? Note which centers are in trouble.

Take up your healing wand. If you can mentally change the color issuing from the tip, do so. If you find this difficult, try placing a dial or switch for the colors on the handle of the wand. Then you can simply set the dial to the chakra color needed.

Set the wand for the color red. Aim the crystal tip at the root center and release the flow of color until the center responds positively. Changing the color to match each chakra, move up the line of light centers, ending at the crown of the head.

Finish by offering the patient a glass of the liquid healing light. When you return to the physical, make your notes as usual.

Diagnosing in the Astral

All illness and disease first appear in the aura. Therefore, all healing must take place first in the aura, then work its way to the physical body. That is why healing can be undone by the patient. If the patient subconsciously doesn't want to be healed because she/he would lose control over the family, for instance, then the person can reject the healing before it goes from the aura into the body.

The first thing any healer must do is determine the truth behind an existing illness. Try talking to the patient to see if she/he knows what is behind any problems. If the person doesn't know, or doesn't want to face the root of the trouble, the healer might have to look into the patient's Akashic records. I don't suggest this unless the healer is pretty certain that the patient will be open to some hard facts.

If the sick person is one who habitually doesn't take responsibility, the healer is probably fighting a losing battle. This type of patient, like the one who really doesn't want to be healed, will undermine your every effort. So the healer comes face to face with an old question: to heal or not to heal. Why waste your energy on a recalcitrant person when others might benefit?

Kirlian photography proves that when you change your thoughts, your energy field or aura changes. Therefore, we are faced with the fact that thoughts have actuality and being. This means that not only do our changing emotional thoughts change our aura, but it is indeed possible for the thoughts of others to affect us. Thoughts can be either negative or positive. Cosmic energy has no rules about how it can be formed. It is merely available to everyone, regardless of their morals.

If you can remain calm and balanced at all times, the negative thoughts of others have little possibility of influencing your aura. However, the catch here is the phrase "at all times." Humans simply don't stay balanced and calm 100 percent of the time. Generally we are in contact with others through relationships, a job, schooling, or in crowds with the very people who are making us not calm and at the same time contaminating our auras.

We are taught to stifle our emotions and logically view and control the situation. Expecting your intellect to totally control your emotions is like your hands telling your circulatory system how to operate. It just doesn't work.

Many people believe in the power of positive thinking. Certainly thinking positively is better than thinking negatively, but here again, you are expecting your intellect to influence your subconscious mind. All positive thinking can do is create a better climate for use of the astral, which comes through the subconscious mind, bypassing the conscious mind altogether.

Naturally, the more positive you can be, the better the results. Negative-minded people show little or no response to astral healing. With those who do show a little improvement, they tend to begin regressing immediately.

Astral Work VI

Trying to change a person's negative attitude is very difficult, but it is possible in some cases. This type of healing works best on those who have recently undergone a traumatic experience. However, if you are faced with a person who has been habitually negative all her/his life, you will have little effect on the person's mental patterns.

Call your patient into your astral healing center. Work on the patient's aura and light centers, removing debris and repairing the damage as much as you can.

Try talking to the person about the damage her/his negative attitude is doing. Have the patient lie on the table and tune your overhead lights to a calming, healing pink, blue, or green. Call for soothing music to fill the room. Wrap the person in a blanket of a healing color. If the patient is still resistant or unresponsive, recommend that she/he spend some quiet time in the worship area before leaving.

Don't feel that you are obligated to expend vast quantities of healing energy if the patient won't listen to you or cooperate. Don't let the occasional failure dent your ego. Everyone has free will to be healed or not.

Healing While on the Astral

To heal yourself or another during your astral-dreams, think about the ailment or problem before sleep. Then begin visualizing the disease shrinking until it disappears. As you drift off to sleep, know that the healing will take place. You will probably find yourself continuing this work during your astral-dreams.

With this method you can contact the astral body of the ill person and influence the person to create changes in her/his aura. Hold the image of the patient in your mind as you fall asleep. Sometimes the only information needed is the name, sex, and age of the patient, and perhaps the person's location. On the astral planes, this appears to be adequate. Deliberately going on an astral journey to perform a healing may be necessary instead of using the astral-dream technique. Once out on the astral planes, call the astral form of the sick person to you. Look at the individual's aura closely. See if you can pinpoint the causes and the extent of the illness. If you cannot determine the cause or have reason to believe that it might extend back into other lifetimes, check into the patient's Akashic records.

Don't assume that this person did something "bad" and is now paying for it. If this were the case, every person on the planet would be dying. Nobody has a perfect Akashic record! Sometimes we bring into this life the subconscious memory patterns of previous diseases because they made such an emotional impact on us before. These memory patterns become activated when we find ourselves in similar situations or once more dealing with people connected to that diseased past life.

The healer must be aware of everything in that past life: the situation that brought about the disease; the people involved who may have contributed to unhappiness, which would foster the growth of such a disease; the mental and emotional attitudes of the afflicted person when the disease manifested.

Sometimes the records will show different diseases striking the same organs or body parts in different lifetimes. This shows a pattern of weakness in that spot. Then the healer must search back in the Akashic records to find the first time the weakness made itself apparent, the causes of that first illness, and again, the people involved. True healing can be a very demanding and time-consuming process.

If past life connections are found, the healer should explain to the astral patient what she/he has uncovered. This is necessary, for the patient must be determined to change her/his thinking and get well. Don't tell your patient in the physical what you have discovered unless you are very certain that your information will be well received. A flat rejection of your information will hamper you in any further attempts at astral healing for that person.

Sometimes the problem is aggravated or even precipitated by other people. Threads from another's aura can be attached to you or others in both the physical or astral planes. This may be done by someone you (or the patient) don't even consider close. You must be aware at all times or you will miss these attacking threads. Strong intentional thoughts, hate, anger, fear, even sight (coupled with any strong emotion) will cause a thread between auras. Strong subconscious desires will also send out threads. For example, if hate is felt by both entities, the threads can be numerous, strong, and difficult to sever.

Persistent, emotionally-backed thoughts use this astral energy to create thoughtforms or bodies. Thoughts are things; never believe they aren't! Thoughtforms have a definite shape and aura of their own. We can either create our own thought-forms of illness and disease, or accept those sent by others.

If the healer, working on the astral, discovers thread attach-ments between the patient and another person, great care must be taken before attempting to sever them. These astral threads are sticky (for lack of a better word). The strongest attachments will ordinarily be at the lower three chakras, particularly the light center found at the solar plexus. These lower chakras are more Earth-connected than the others and more bound up in emotions.

Be certain you know the intent of the threads before undertaking this severing process. There are healthy and positive thread-attachments: between mother and child, lovers, family members, a person and pets, friends. These positive threads will be pure, healthy colors. Negative threads tend to be of dark, muddy colors and give off a burning hot or freezing cold feeling for some distance around.

Once severed, these threads tend to whip around, attaching themselves to any aura in their vicinity. The healer must know how to protect her/himself. Try to discover, if possible, who is sending and maintaining these threads: a physical or an astral being. If it is a physical person, the patient must face the responsibility of breaking contact with that person and then keeping her/his protective guard up until the offending person loses interest. If it is an astral being, try to find out if the patient is a co-perpetrator by keeping this being in her/his thoughts and subconsciously desiring the being's presence. In either case, talk to the patient's astral form and try to convince her/him of the necessity of breaking contact.

Begin your healing-attack by donning a suit of armor or protective gear similar to that used by people investigating toxic spills. The idea is to convince your astral body that it is totally protected, that there are no openings through which the threads can find their way. Take as much time as necessary to visualize this armor in total completeness. Any threads that whip against your protective gear will shrivel and die.

Arm yourself with a sharp sword (for the severing) and a torch or flame-thrower (for cauterization of the thread-stump left attached to the patient). Note to which light centers the threads are attached; this will give you clues as to the emotional origin that set up this situation in the first place.

Call upon positive cosmic light and send it flashing into your sword blade. Swing your sword as hard as you can against the threads. If the threads have been attached for a long time and/or are particularly thick, it may take several cuts to break them loose. Immediately cauterize the thread-stump which will still be attached to the patient. This prevents reattachment.

After this procedure, the patient may experience some slight discomfort or illness in the general area of the attachment. The patient may have a long-standing problem in this area. This occurs only if the patient has been partially to blame for the predicament. To keep the threads from reattaching, suggest that the patient wear a protective amulet for several weeks or even months.

Healing is related to changing the future, in a way. By choosing to be healed, you are directly changing parts of your future which are still elastic in nature. Your astral body has access to the records of your possible future, letting you see which things are crystallized and which are not. Even if you think an illness is crystallized, proceed with the healing. Removal of the problem or disease may come about in a way you didn't check on in the astral.

The Psychical Research Societies have records of predictions, including many about diseases or ill health. Cases where the disease was seen but nothing was done to change the future show that the illness manifested every time. When the predicted disease was treated psychically before its manifestation, the disease either didn't appear or appeared in a modified form.

Hawaiian kahunas believe that the astral body is an exact mold of every cell of the physical body. Because this astral body is made of an invisible, non-physical substance, it cannot be damaged in any way. To repair a damaged physical part, the healer needs to mentally reduce the physical body into astral energy and then reform it according to the mold of the astral body. This can be applied to all diseases. Cancer can be dissolved and reformed into normal, healthy tissue, for example.

Sometimes an illness is connected to a deep sense of sin or guilt. For the healing to be successful, these negative emotions must first be removed. However, the healer cannot do this for the patient, although she/he can bring such deep feelings to the conscious knowledge of the sick person.

In all psychic healing, the subconscious mind must be contacted first. You have to be able to see the subject mentally in order to find and identify the problem. If you don't really want to make this contact, don't try at all. Listen to your intuitive senses. It could be that this person doesn't want to be healed. Perhaps the patient just can't face the fact that she/he has caused the illness for a purely selfish reason. Hostile patients seldom get well. Above all, don't feel that it is your "duty" to heal everyone whose problems are presented to you by the person or someone else.

The subconscious mind is capable of amazing things. Without any conscious thought on our part, it keeps us breathing, our heart beating, our digestive system working, etc. All psychic and auric healing is simply impressing a positive suggestion upon the subconscious mind.

Most states have very strict laws about psychic healing. Obey these laws so you don't court problems with the authorities. Don't diagnose illnesses to the patient; keep your observations quiet and use them for guidance in healing. Don't prescribe anything—herbs, massage, exercises, anything. And don't physically touch a patient, unless she/he is a like believer and very close friend. In some states, the laying on of hands is enough to get you thrown in jail. Orthodox religions feel that psychic healers are treading in their sacred territory when this is done and will joyfully do their "duty" by reporting you to the authorities. Doctors aren't any better on this point. Besides, in this day of crying "sexual harassment" at the slightest provocation, it is safest to keep your hands to yourself.

Astral Work VII

Diagnosing an actual physical, mental, or emotional illness from the astral planes takes some creative thinking. For one thing, illnesses often do not reveal themselves astrally in the same manner as they do physically. It doesn't really matter if you can put a medical name to the problem you see while astral healing. What does matter is that you reverse or remove the immediate problem, plus get at the roots of what is causing it.

When you have journeyed to your astral healing space and your patient has arrived, go through several diagnostic procedures to determine if you are correctly assessing the problem.

Start by viewing the patient's aura and light centers while she/he is standing against your blank white wall. Carefully note all the potential trouble spots you see: flares, tears, changes in color, symbols, dark spots. Run your hands through the patient's aura to detect any hot and/or cold areas.

Next, talk to the patient. Listen to what the person says and how she/he says it. This conversation may well hold vital clues to the roots of the problems: relationships, stress, self-doubts, feelings of guilt or sin, and so on. If possible, have the patient go to the worship area of the healing temple for a while so you can talk to the person's teacher-guides. Again, listen carefully to what is said. If necessary, look through the patient's Akashic records and trace back the continuing disturbances.

When your patient returns to your "office," have her/him relax on the table or in the chair. Put on a pair of x-ray goggles or glasses. With these you can look through layers of body tissue, much like a CAT-scan does. Check out the circulatory and digestive systems, the kidneys and bladder, all the lymph glands, etc. Note any restrictions in the flow of body fluids, any dark masses or unusual patterns, and any breaks in the flow of bodily electrical energies.

Illnesses manifest themselves differently on the astral than they do in the physical. Some diseases will emit an insect-like chattering noise. Kidney and bladder infections often appear as a black sludge clogging up the system. Blood diseases or infections may show up as too many white spots floating in the red blood. Narrowed blood vessels may emit a laboring sucking sound instead of the ordinary swish-swish of circulation. With a little practice and close attention, the healer will begin to understand how diseases and imbalances present themselves to her/him.

Keep notes about each diagnosis. You will begin to see a recurring pattern which will help you to pinpoint certain diseases immediately.

Working on Yourself

Regular realignment of your own psychic bodies is an important task for any healer. Ordinary happenings in life are enough to throw one or more of these bodies out of alignment, but as a healer you are working with the negative astral influences of others, which can misalign your bodies even quicker.

Most of us do better at keeping ourselves healthy under trying circumstances than we think. Our astral bodies are in constant attunement with the vast cosmic energy which makes up the universe and everything in it. This cosmic energy also extends onto Otherworld planes of existence. Our astral bodies are set up to automatically protect and repair themselves, thus keeping the physical, mental, and emotional bodies in good health, too. Our problems begin when we are constantly bombarded with negative vibrations by our own thinking and from those around us, even casual passers-by.

The cause of most illnesses is that we systematically and regularly abuse our bodies. Our automatic repair system (the aura and the chakras) is so efficient that we can get away with this for years before the repair system gives up or breaks down. Disease then becomes evident through the squeezed off flow of incoming psychic energy. Ordinarily, this energy dissolves congestions and obstructions before they become a danger.

Only a small part of the emotion you feel is self-generated, or your own. Emotions are easily transferred from one person to another, most of the time without the receiver being aware of what is happening. The first step in understanding a sudden wave of negative emotions is to determine whether they are self-generated or are coming from someone else.

Some people with very serious problems, such as alcohol and drug addiction, are extremely difficult, if not impossible, to heal. This is because their problems are not basically emotionally derived. Their main problems stem from a lack of self-discipline and self-mastery.

Astral Work VIII

The hardest healing there will ever be is on the healer her/himself. This is because most of the healing must be derived first from introspection and facing facts.

153

Go to your astral healing space and call upon your healing teacher. If one hasn't appeared to you yet, this is the perfect time to send out an emergency call. When this healing guide does appear, spend some time getting acquainted with her/him. You may discover that you have one main healing teacher, with several others on call.

View your aura and light centers in the mirror. Be very honest about what you see. Rejection of any problems will only hurt you and set back your progress. During this diagnosis time, your teacher or teachers will probably take an active part in the healing process. Clean your aura, making any necessary repairs. Strengthen and adjust your light centers with your healing wand. Remove any unnatural objects from your auric body. Patch any "holes" in the auric form and the aura itself. Sit in blue, pink, or green light for a time to accelerate the healing process.

If your healing teachers indicate that they will work on you, sit back and relax. Listen to their advice, and note any changes they suggest. Of course, run this advice through common sense when you return to the physical body, but do give it honest consideration. You may be too close to the problem to see it for what it actually is.

Various Healing Techniques

A good and conscientious healer will use whatever visual healing methods she/he finds that work. Some physical healing techniques can be adopted to astral healing by creative visualization.

Many ancient peoples, including the Egyptians, were believers of healing by other than pure physical methods. They thought that the mind and astral body were capable of creating perfect forms of being, then bringing that perfected form into the physical. So both physical and astral healing were considered essential to a lasting healing of the body.

In Europe, there have been studies of the effect of certain types of music on healing. These investigators believe that this music has a direct influence on the subconscious mind, a step up from most of the similar studies done in the United States. They say that this occurs by transforming the sounds into direct vibrations which affect the cellular tissue. Bach fugues have been used to treat indigestion; Mozart to treat rheumatism; Beethoven to treat hernias; Schubert to treat insomnia; and Handel to treat depression, despondency, and disturbed emotional states.

This impact of certain tones and music upon the physical body is important whether or not you are sick. This may be because certain types of music affect the emotions, which in turn affect both the astral and physical bodies. Consider using calming music in your astral healing space.

Using a pyramid form for physical healing along with astral treatment of the aura has proved beneficial in the treatment of pain. For a headache or other pain, place a small pyramid of wood or even cardboard on the forehead or wherever the physical pain is centered. Leave the pyramid there for about five minutes.

Pyramid power is a fascinating subject in itself. The energy emanating from pyramids obviously has greater uses than keeping razor blades sharp. We are still relearning the uses of this energy. Be very cautious, however, about using pyramids over the light centers in either the physical or astral bodies. Their energy is so strong that it is easy to get the covered chakra emitting far too much power.

Be sure to consider the use of gems and stones in the astral to bring about a healing. Such devices, if properly used, will amplify and focus the power of the healer. Study such tools before using them astrally, for their uses on both planes of existence usually are the same.

Certain stones have long been associated with specific powers as well as with the light centers. In the physical, it is often financially impossible to own all the stones you would like. In the astral realms, this is no problem. Match the color of the stone to the color of the chakra if you can't remember exactly which one is needed. Rose quartz, in both the physical and astral, tends to speed up chakra activity, while tourmaline tends to be calming.

Many people have the mistaken idea that mesmerism is the same as hypnotism. Franz Anton Mesmer believed that the body has certain energy paths for the transference of energy. When these paths become blocked, illness results. These paths seem much like the light centers and the paths known in acupuncture.

He discovered that stroking the body with magnets could remove the blockages and allow the energy to flow again as it should.

Using magnets in astral healing is valuable if you detect that the energy currents of the body are weak, disrupted, or even too strong. The carriers of electrical energy in the body are the nerves. In hyperactive children and nervous adults you will find this energy is "wild" in places and almost choked off in others.

The Celtic Scots and Irish have healers who, they say, are given their powers by faeries through visits to the Otherworlds. These healers use healing charms and a prayer called the *seachd phaidir* (literally, the seventh prayer). The words of this prayer change from person to person, and it usually is not divulged to anyone. The words are whispered over the diseased area of the body, then the healer "charms" the sickness out of the body and into another person, animal, tree, hill, or stone. This belief is so strong in the Highlands of Scotland that those visiting a sick person won't enter the house unless a dog goes in first.

This whispered prayer and charm are considered to be so effective that they can be spoken into a piece of cloth. The cloth can then be taken miles away, tied about the diseased or injured body part, and the charm will work.

Prayer, however it is said, can be very effective. When you are working in the astral with a person who believes in prayer, choose your words and the deity name according to the patient's personal religious beliefs. When you send the patient to the worship area of the healing temple, you need not fear the person will be offended by anything that is in opposition to her/his belief. This worship area will adjust itself, visually and vibrationally, to meet the needs of any worshippers.

Astral Work IX

Using different techniques often becomes the only option the healer has to get through to and make a positive impression upon the patient's subconscious mind.

Often healers in the astral will use specific essential oils to seal the light centers just before the patient returns to the physical.

To do this, place a dab of the oil on your forefinger and gently put a touch of it on each chakra, beginning with the root center and ending at the crown of the head. Each chakra has certain oils which vibrate at its rate.

Magnets, as discussed above, can be useful in correcting any irregular electrical energy flows through the nerves. When using magnets in healing, stroke the body from the head down through the trunk and out each arm and leg to the tips of the fingers and toes. You are gently working the energy from its source to the extremities of the nerves.

To use a pyramid, either set a small one directly over a painful or diseased area, or have the patient sit under a large one for a short period of time for over-all balancing.

Never cut or tear anything out of the astral body. Remember, you are creating something in the astral which will eventually manifest in the physical. Pluck foreign objects out of the aura or astral form with tweezers or your fingers. Sometimes you will find an object impossible to remove. This may be because the patient doesn't want to be healed or the person has become so attached to the problem that she/he doesn't know how to release it. The only option the healer has in cases such as this is to encapsulate the disease or object.

Mix some of the astral putty with the liquid light. Completely cover the disease with this mixture, giving it the instructions that as it hardens it will shrink and so will the disease within it. Whether or not you succeed in eliminating the disease will be up to the patient. But you have encapsulated the problem to keep it from growing and spreading.

The transplantation of organs and body limbs is not advisable on the astral. Doctors don't even have much success with this procedure in the physical. Instead, use your healing wand to dissolve the diseased or damaged part into a liquid. Run it through a sieve to remove any abnormal cells. Reform it into a healthy, perfectly functioning part and replace it in the body.

If the diseased or damaged organ or part is a result of past life troubles, the patient will need to face what happened and forgive her/himself and any others involved. If it is the result of a past life injury, the patient needs to release the emotions linked with that life and the event that caused the injury. This look at past lives will only work, of course, with those who believe they had such past lives.

It is a good idea, even when working on yourself, to periodically flush toxins out of the astral body. While in your astral healing space, the patient can be hooked up to intravenous tubes which inject a blood purifier, or large quantities of liquid light can be poured through the mouth and allowed to work through the intestinal and urinary tracts.

Healing and purifying by the use of colored light therapy is another method to clean out the astral body and the aura. The patient can sit in a chair while being bathed with a specific color of light, or the person may be more comfortable wrapped in a blanket of the appropriate shade. I have one friend who likes to visualize a hot tub with the appropriate colored water; he soaks in this until he feels better.

Aligning the various bodies of a patient, or yourself, is also necessary for balance and healing. Each person has several astral bodies: the mental, emotional, and spiritual, plus the general astral form which acts as a vehicle for all of them. They all get out of alignment on occasion. This can happen because of negative or traumatic events or, in the case of the astral body, of a too sudden return from a journey.

Realigning your own astral bodies is basically the same method used to realign those of a patient. First, look in the mirror to see what form is not in its proper place. This will appear as a blur in the aura or as two or more body-shapes overlapping.

Begin by pulling all the forms up above the crown center at the top of the head. Mentally call for the astral body. Take its form and pull it down over the physical shape like putting on a glove. Smooth it down as much as possible. Repeat this with the mental, the emotional, and finally the spiritual forms. Having these bodies in correct alignment is an excellent precaution against succumbing to incoming negative thoughtforms as well as correcting energy flows and resisting diseases.

Eleven

Magick in the Astral

Almost all people who desire to learn about magick, or who have taken the plunge and work with it, have experienced magickal endeavors in past lives. Some practiced magick more than others, but you wouldn't be interested today if you hadn't had a taste of magick in another lifetime. You can still tap into that past discipline, confidence, and expertise, bringing it to life once more in your subconscious mind so you can draw upon it when you wish. Old skills, magickal or otherwise, are available if you can learn to access them.

Delving into your Akashic records in the astral is the only way to find out about past lives connected in some way with magickal endeavors. You may have directly used magick, or you may have been in a Mystery religion that touched on the fringes of magick. Either way, you have had valuable skills that can benefit you in this lifetime. You can use these skills to build a better life for yourself.

Beware of anyone telling you not to use magick to help yourself to a better life. That is simply a trap to keep you under control. Using magick is one of the big "Thou shalt nots" of orthodox religions. Knowing how to use magick means you can become an independent person, no longer dependent upon others for guidance in everyday or spiritual life. Yes, magick does lead to greater spirituality, for the very roots of all positive magick lie in a belief in a Supreme Creator and a spiritual afterlife.

Many people would love to practice magick, but they feel they aren't intelligent enough or need a physical guru. This isn't true. Patience, practice, and a belief in yourself is what is really essential for the practice of magick. Remember, if you think you can or you think you can't, you're right! Confidence and a feeling of worthiness are the keys to effective magick.

You need to create a mental pattern of winning. To do this, start your magickal endeavors on small things and work up to the big ones. In this way you gain experience in how to correctly work magick, but even more importantly, you gain the confidence that you actually can do magick.

The ancient Egyptians believed that the mind had the power to set vibrations in motion which would eventually manifest in the physical. They also said that humans were made up of the same elemental forces which were used to build the universe; the Egyptians called these forces the seven astral rays. This is simply another way of describing unlimited astral energy, which is the foundation of all creation.

Since only 10 percent of your potential and power are available to you in your regular state of consciousness, you need to go into the astral planes to tap the remaining 90 percent. If you limit yourself to physically working magick, you are not using the most powerful part of your mind.

There are definite differences between physical and astral magick. Physical magick requires actual physical and mental work; the request must pass from the physical realm into the astral to be manifested before it can return as the desired result.

Astral magick is much more difficult and demanding, but can also be more effective and show results much quicker. The magician has to know how to get onto the astral planes and set up her/his ritual area. Astral magick requires complete visualization right down to the senses. You have to learn how to handle and control astral energies and shape them into the form you desire so that they can then manifest in the physical. You have to be very specific in astral magick, or you will get mixed results in the manifestation.

If this sounds daunting, don't be afraid to try astral magick. After all, you have worked at astral healing. Astral magick is just a more in-depth and intense training.

If you are having difficulty pulling your consciousness out of the physical body along with the separation of the astral body from the physical, you might try visualizing a vortex of swirling energy pointing down at the top of your head. Let this vortex lift you up out of your body. You will still have the cord connection and the ability to return whenever you wish.

Astral Magick I

As always, decide where you want to go and what you want to do before you begin your astral journey. In this exercise, you want to specify that you go to an astral area suitable for erecting your ritual temple and performing magick.

Building your astral magickal ritual area will probably take more than one journey into the astral realms. The beauty of an astral magickal temple is that you can make it as simple or as complex as you wish. What you cannot afford in your physical magickal temple has no bearing upon what you can have in its astral equivalent. Money isn't the medium of exchange in the astral; concentration, patience, and hard work are.

Go out into the astral as you usually do. If you have expressed the desire to arrive at an appropriate place to build your magickal temple, you will find yourself in that spot. You may find your astral lover, teacher-guides, and perhaps some long-gone magicians waiting to help you.

Begin your work by visualizing the structure of your special place. Don't worry about the furnishings at this point. Concentrate upon the way the temple is formed. Make it out of certain woods or stone. Project a big enough main room for magickal ceremonies. Smaller adjoining rooms can be used for storing quantities of herbs, oils, stones, and magickal equipment. Set aside a study where you can relax before and after rituals, and collect such additional things as copies of ancient magickal books. Work at the visualization of this magickal temple until you can see every detail of the architecture. Wander through all the rooms until you know the floor plan of the entire astral structure. Use your hands to feel the wood or stone. Smell the clean scents of this new building.

Color the rooms in the shades you want; add tapestries, draperies, rugs, paintings, and windows. Don't neglect the exterior. Build your temple in any shape or architectural design you want. Surround it with gardens and a stream, or set it high on a rocky mountain. This is your chance to perform your magick in what you might consider to be an ideal setting.

When you are satisfied with the results of your imaging, begin to furnish your temple according to your desires. Leave the main ritual room until last as you will be expending vast amounts of time and energy to get everything right there. Begin with the smaller rooms. For example, stock the shelves in your store rooms with herbs, oils, candles, incense, and spring water. You can create exotic-shaped glass containers or replicas of ancient chests.

One of these rooms should be a dressing room with a closet and full-length mirror. In this closet you can put any number of ritual robes or dresses. You can create them in a variety of styles and colors, each suitable for a different type of ceremony or your mood at the time. These can be plain or decorated. In this dressing room have a chest which will hold any jewelry you may want to wear. If you plan to wear shoes of any kind, create these and place them in the closet with the robes.

Move on to your study. Furnish this room with a desk and shelves of books. Include a comfortable chair for reading and any other furnishings you think you might need or want. Be sure to install some kind of lighting in each room.

Finally, move into your main ritual area. Take your time creating it in just the way you want. Place an altar or large table in the center. If you want, set up statues around the sides of the room. Position candle holders where you think they will be of the most use. If at a later date you decide that something in the temple isn't exactly how you want it to be, specifically erase the parts you want removed and visualize new ones.

Although you needn't create every single ritual tool you may want to use at this time, it is best to carefully create those you know you will need in most ceremonies: wand, dagger, sword, incense burner, chalice, cauldron, and of course a book containing your favorite rituals. Either lay each tool on the altar or on a table at one side of the ritual room.

If you like soft appropriate background music, create something to provide this. If you're using lighting other than candles, create something to dim the lights at your command. Become familiar and comfortable with your astral magickal temple.

As your final act for this journey, call upon your teacher-guides to join you in your magickal temple. Listen to their advice and suggestions. They will make suggestions, but never order you to change anything. Thank them for their help and exit the astral journey as usual.

Astral Magicians and Teachers

There are wise teachers, masters, and highly advanced spiritual beings who can show you how to do great magickal things on the astral. While in the astral, or on any astral journey, it is possible to contact and talk with knowledgeable people from any part of history.

The biggest concern of new astral travelers and workers is how to determine if an entity is positive or negative. All astral entities and spirit beings have auras. Look closely at these auras to determine what the colors and symbols say to you. Also open up your intuitive senses. Are you comfortable, uncomfortable, or merely want to get away as fast as you can? When the aura of an astral or spirit being makes contact with your own aura when you are in the physical, you immediately have a feeling of not being alone. When you are out on the astral, you can see the auras of these beings as well as feel the true emotional intents coming from them.

Don't assume you automatically know who an astral being is. They will tell you who and what they are if you ask. This applies to deities, as well as to other entities. Don't fall for the erroneous idea that calling a negative entity by its name will compel it to do good. All beings, astral or physical, are true to their nature.

When auras (in the physical or in the astral) come in contact with each other, they feed emotions and data to the various individuals through the subconscious mind. All communication is through telepathy.

If you have a positive attitude, trust in the protection of your teachers and lover, and know your own worth, you won't be unduly influenced through this exchange of information, even if the entity is negative. If you aren't sure about an astral entity, check on the emotions you are feeling from the being. If the feelings are negative, remove yourself from its vicinity. Don't fall victim to feelings of fear, as this will give negative entities a type of control over you. Be indignant that these negative beings should be bothering you at all! Order them to leave, call upon your teacher-guides, and go about your business.

Astral Magick II

Studying under an astral magician can be an exciting and informative experience. Go out onto the astral planes and move directly to your magickal temple. When you are comfortably seated at your desk in your study, put out a mental call for an astral magician who can help you learn to use astral magick.

When you first do this, it is better not to specify a magician by name. I do suggest not calling upon any ancient magician who had even a tinge of negativity about her/him. You might want to discuss your choice with your regular teacher-guides and let them guide you to a person they feel is suitable.

If you feel hesitant about meeting this magician, ask one of your teachers to be with you when the person arrives. Introduce yourself and state why you have called upon her/him. Even though the magician will know instantly, the period of instruction will go better if you can express your intentions.

Listen closely to what the magician says. She/he may well begin with some basic magickal instructions of working on the astral planes. After this brief introduction, the magician will go with you into the main ritual area. There you will be shown how to call to you, handle, and mold astral energy.

As you stand before your altar, call for creative astral energy to gather in your hands. At this point, you do not want to have any particular result in mind. You are simply gathering the energy. The astral energy will form a glowing ball of light between your hands. It will feel both hot and cold, tingly, and very much alive in its own way.

Mold this energy into a compact ball as you would moist clay. Keep shaping and molding the energy until it is perfectly round and compact. For this exercise you will be creating a crystal ball. As you hold the molded energy, visualize a beautiful crystal ball in your hands. Don't see this energy turning into a crystal ball, but *as* a crystal ball. There is a difference. Seeing something turning into something else requires a lengthy, often abortive, procedure. Seeing something *as* something else requires the energy to make an immediate metamorphosis into what you are visualizing. If your visualization is flawed, so will be your creation. So hold your visualization until the creation is complete.

When the astral energy has formed itself into a crystal ball, place it in a holder or in a velvet-lined box for safe keeping. You will find that either the magician or your teacher has created such a holder or box for you while you were working. This is a good example of how methodical you must be in working astral magick: consider absolutely everything you need before you begin.

Spend as much time talking with the magician as you wish. When you are ready to leave your journey, thank the person for her/his help and return as usual. You may find that you study with a different magician each time you do this particular astral journey. Magicians tend to excel in one specific area of magick

165

above all others, so multiple teachers in the field of magick will be to your benefit.

"Terror of the Threshold"

There is a term in the occult field used to describe a frightening but benevolent entity: the "Terror of the Threshold." This astral guardian keeps you from getting in over your head because you are indecisive and fearful. This being will appear in the form that frightens you most. Coming face to face with it can be terrifying. You have to pass the test and overcome your fear before you can advance. When you have faced this guardian in the proper manner, it will transform into a totally different being. If it doesn't transform, you can be certain that you have some deeply buried fears and preconceptions that need to be unearthed.

Every astral magician has to pass by this Terror before she/he can perform really effective magick on the astral planes or learn some of the ancient mystical secrets. One of the biggest fears of astral traveling is contacting non-physical entities. Once you break through the fear barrier of contacting and working with spirit beings, you gain the reward of greater effectiveness in any work you do while on the astral. Contacting the Terror can be especially difficult, because this entity reflects all our deepest fears in its appearance.

Some potential magicians are never able to come to terms with this entity guarding the threshold to greater subconscious depths and power. These people are simply unable or unwilling to overcome the negative propaganda about the astral and magick with which they have been contaminated. Success or failure of this ultimate magickal-spiritual experience rests totally on the shoulders of the magician.

No one else can do anything to get you past the Terror of the Threshold. The right to pass can only occur through your accepting personal responsibility and doing what is necessary, releasing old programmed fears and lies. You are the only person who is responsible for what positive or negative ideas and information are in your mind.

This so-called Terror has another duty once you have passed over the threshold. It guards your physical body from being disturbed or harassed by astral entities and also keeps such beings from challenging you upon your return. The Terror is a powerful ally for all astral healers and magicians.

Successfully meeting, talking with, and passing the Terror of the Threshold is one of the astral initiations through which every astral magician must pass if she/he would really be successful with magick.

Astral Magick III

Go out onto the astral planes as usual. If you want, you can make a stop at your astral temple first. Spending a little time here will help you gather your courage for the upcoming meeting with the Terror of the Threshold.

Suddenly you are moving along a darkened path through a tangled forest. Soon you move out of the forest and into a clearing before the gates of a great golden castle. Before the closed gates of this wonderful structure stands a giant figure. This figure (whose form may be frightening) bars your way with fierce gestures. Since this entity is built out of personal inner fears, there is no way to describe it. Everyone's experiences with the Terror will be different.

Now you must call upon all your magickal power to determine what makes up this entity. Ask it a series of questions to get it to reveal its nature. This will not be easy because your own subconscious mind, which created this Terror in the first place, will try to avoid revealing the truth behind its appearance. The questions should be specific, such as "Are you made from my fears of death?", "Are you composed out of propaganda about hell and the devil?", or "Are you my fears of failure and being wrong?" Keep at the questioning until you get answers. It is quite likely that this personal Terror is built out of any number of hidden fears, not just one.

With each question that touches upon the truth, you must consider if you still believe that way or are simply holding on to old programming. If it touches upon a personal trait, habit, or problem, have you dealt with it or do you honestly plan to face it? With each positive decision you make, the Terror will begin to change.

Sometimes the confrontation is too much to be resolved in a single meeting. You can only retreat and try again at another time. Other times, this entity will let you pass although there are a few unsolved problems to face. For this to happen, you must know the problems, face their existence, and be prepared to do something about them.

Don't ever expect that one such confrontation with the Terror will be your last. We humans are always destroying old mental negativities and replacing them with new ones. That is why a good astral magician must always be alert to the negatives that pop up in her/his thoughts.

If you are allowed to pass through the gates of this golden castle, your experiences within will be intensely personal, individualized, and therefore unexplainable. Each visit will likely present you with a new spiritual experience, for this golden castle is the initiation center for astral magicians. Both ceremonial magicians and followers of Wicca usually have a progression through various degrees or levels of status. It is the same in this castle.

Your first experience will be one of initiation into being a full-fledged astral magician. You will be at the bottom of the ladder, so to speak, but the rate of progression only depends upon your efforts, dedication, and willingness to learn from the more advanced entities and travelers of the astral planes. No one can put in a good word and get you to the next level of initiation before you are qualified.

When you leave the castle, you will find the Terror waiting for you. Because it has been guarding your physical body, it will help you return quickly and easily to the physical plane.

Psychic Talents

Psychic states of altered consciousness produce heightened awareness of all the senses, physical and non-physical. Going into an altered state of consciousness, or astral traveling, will help you with the development of all forms of what are called psychic talents. Astral travel appears to sensitize the traveler to the flows of astral energies and what is being created and has been created in them.

Even if your meditative state isn't very deep, allow whatever pictures come to play themselves across your mind's eye. Creative people often do this automatically, without any training or interest in the occult field. Robert Louis Stevenson said that he got all his stories clairvoyantly. He simply let his characters play out their scenes in his mind while he watched.

Ancient cultures have always associated the development of psychic talents with the third eye in the center of the forehead. This light center is connected with the pineal gland.

The tiny pineal gland lies approximately in the center of the brain. In some creatures, such as a certain New Zealand lizard, this gland appears to be a non-functioning vestigial eye. The pineal gland secretes the chemical serotonin, one of the naturally produced chemicals which produces a "high." The secretion of serotonin is greater during meditation and altered states of consciousness than at any other time. You might even call serotonin a "psychic hormone."

Psychic abilities are naturally strengthened through astral travel. They can also be deliberately strengthened by magick performed while on the astral. Such talents as intuition, clairvoyance, clairaudience, precognition, telepathy, telekinesis, psychometry, and dowsing can be enhanced and more fully developed through magickal means on the astral planes.

Telekinesis means to move things without touching them, a state of mind over matter. Dr. J. B. Rhine of Duke University conducted a series of experiments on this, as well as other psychic abilities, in the mid-1930s. People with this ability can move pencils, influence compass needles and calculators, and cause floating corks to change direction. I've never found a practical use for this ability in the physical.

Psychometry is the ability to read the history of an object by touching it. Joseph Rodes Buchanan, a professor of medicine at Cincinnati Medical School in the mid-1800s, did some psychometry experiments with his students and had great success with them. Buchanan decided that our nerves give off an electrical field (the aura) which conveys a symbolic history of the object to our minds. William Denton, a professor of geology at Boston College, later ran experiments with geological samples wrapped in paper. Denton came to the conclusion that everything in nature can be imprinted in some way with its history, and that a part of the human mind is capable of reading this imprinted history. Obviously, this ability does not lie in the logical left brain, but in the psychic right brain.

Psychometry can be used to read the history and sometimes the future connected with objects, such as jewelry, stones, or pottery. This information is in the form of vibrations caused by traumatic natural events or events in the lives of people who handle or wear the objects. Plastics, leather, cloth, and paper do not seem to hold vibrations; it is ordinarily not possible to get any information out of objects made of these materials.

Precognition sometimes comes in flashes of "knowing" or in prophetic dreams. In using precognition to know the future, place the question clearly in your mind. Don't expect an immediate answer to your questions. Relax, let the conscious mind become occupied with something, and the answer will pop through from the subconscious mind.

Clairaudience means to hear inwardly; religion calls this the voice of spirit. This can mean hearing a disembodied voice with the physical ears or hearing and understanding an astral voice with the inner ears.

Clairvoyance means clear seeing. The Celts called this the Second Sight. People with this ability can see spirits and entities in the spirit world. It also enables the astral traveler to see clearly while out on the astral planes. Most of the time clairvoyance operates as seeing within the mind's eye, but sometimes it opens up to an actual physical seeing. For most people, this physical seeing occurs as flashes of movement or things seen in the peripheral vision, but if one turns to look straight at the movement, there is nothing.

Telepathy is the ability to send a mental message from one person to another. When two people have strong connections, they can easily send and receive messages. Sometimes the sending appears to only go in one direction, with one person only sending and the other only receiving. Some animals become quite good at this, too. Next time your cat sits and stares at you, see if you are receiving a message of an empty food dish or the desire to go outside.

Dowsing, or the finding of underground water, pipes, or tanks, is a fun and interesting occupation. Some people use pendulums, others willow wands or bent coat hangers. During the Vietnam War, underground bunkers were uncovered by dowsing with bent metal rods.

Intuition appears to be emotionally based and connected with the solar plexus. Sometimes it is called a "gut feeling." It is an instant knowing that something should or should not be done. Did you ever get a feeling that you shouldn't sign a contract, be friends with or date a person, or make a decision in a certain way? Then you went ahead and did whatever it was anyway and regretted it. That was your intuition speaking. It is probably the most commonly developed of the psychic talents.

Crystal gazing to see either into the future or past can be used both on the physical and astral. While gazing into the crystal, hold in mind an image of the person or event you want to check on. Scrying, or crystal gazing, is a very ancient magickal art. However, crystals were not always used by the seer. The kahunas of Hawaii used black stones in containers of water. Other cultures have used goblets of water, pools of ink, blank white walls, or shiny reflective objects set on a black cloth.

Reading tarot cards or runes is much like crystal gazing. Almost anyone can memorize what cards or runes mean, but not everyone can put the finishing psychic touches on a reading. Using tools, such as tarot cards and runes, appears to touch upon a combination of psychic talents: psychometry, precognition, intuition, and clairvoyance.

The Celts believed that the faery folk were in constant contact with future possibilities. If a person attracted and worked with a Co-walker, or faery companion, that person could become a seer, or one who "sees" into the future. Often these seers used the technique of looking through a knothole or a ring in order to get a better view of the Otherworlds and their faery companions. The same effect can be produced by forming a small tunnel with the slightly clenched fingers of your hand. As you look through this tunnel, you will be able to see psychic pictures against the darkened area of the hand.

Among the Celts and many other religious traditions, tears or watering of the eyes was considered to be a sign of true prophetic ability. Authentic trance mediums will often have tears running from their eyes while they are working. I've seen tarot readers who reached such a borderline state between the physical and the astral that their eyes began to tear.

The Scottish seers spoke of a terrifying sight when the Second Sight is first used: astral entities seem to rush toward the seer from all directions. This seems logical, since astral entities of all types want to be recognized. When they discover someone who has learned how to see into the astral, these beings rush from all directions for recognition. This can be a little over-whelming, rather like being the new kid in school. Meeting crowds of astral beings is also quite common when you first go into deep meditation. Just stand your ground and feel confident about your abilities. They will back off as soon as they realize you know what you are doing.

The Celts also taught that seers who had positive thoughts and deeds attracted positive Otherworld companions, while those harboring negative thoughts and deeds drew only negative beings. The Celts also believed that if a person did something negative, the Co-walker would leave. We might call this Co-walker a teacher-guide. Since one attracts like vibrational entities, it is logical that the higher teacher would leave if the person's vibrations drop into the negative range.

Astral Magick IV

When developing psychic talents, the magician can either go to her/his magickal temple or enter an astral class given by an advanced astral being. Either way, the astral training is basically the same: practice, patience, and understanding that you can do it. When back in the physical, strengthen your astral learning by physical practice in each of these areas.

Create any tools you might need for developing these abilities. You already created a crystal ball. Use the same techniques for manifesting tarot cards or runes, a pendulum or rods for dowsing, etc. For talents which do not require tools, you will need one-on-one training with a teacher.

When studying telekinesis, visualize a compass. Try to make the compass needle turn in a specific direction. When you first try this, expect the needle to do everything but what you want. This is a good exercise for sharpening your concentration and determination.

Intuition, clairvoyance, clairaudience, precognition, and telepathy are learned, even in the astral, by constantly practicing and learning to open your mind to the answers. Be sure you separate the true and actual answers from what you would like them to be. Being honest with yourself is very important.

A teacher will likely practice sending telepathic thoughts with you in a one-on-one situation. Since astral entities communicate in this way, the practice of telepathy is important. Clairvoyance and clairaudience are greatly improved once you establish a strong telepathic communication link with an astral being. In strengthening intuition, the teacher may help you by sensitizing your solar plexus light center. Precognition usually comes through prophetic dreams. Your teacher may work on your astral body to be more receptive to these, then follow the procedure with vivid dreams of little things out of the future. The best way to recognize these dreams as prophetic is to keep a dream journal in which you date and record your nightly experiences.

For dowsing, your teacher will probably have you walk over an area with a pendulum or rods to determine a hidden object "underground." You will go through a series of tests finding different substances until you intuitively know the "feel" of the various materials.

Crystal gazing and reading tarot cards or runes will be a matter of practice and more practice, both in the astral and in the physical. Your teacher will help you with interpretations, while at the same time teaching you the method which is best for you.

Actual practice of these talents is the most common method of instruction by an astral teacher. This instructor will sit beside you while you gaze into the crystal or lay out the tarot cards or runes. Then she/he will help you with interpretation. Good and vivid astral sight is important in order for you to completely understand what your astral teacher is telling you.

Choose only one psychic talent at a time to work on. Schedule at least two weekly deliberate astral journeys to practice this talent. Your instructor will tell you when to proceed to the next talent.

Shaping Astral Energy

The very air we breathe is full of astral energy, or as the Hindus call it, prana. It is this energy that flows into all our light centers, opens the third eye, and creates or manifests our intense desires or fears. Energy from the astral planes can be deliberately molded and reshaped in any form you wish. Astral energy is unlimited, has no preconceived positive or negative powers, and is available to anyone. This energy also can be molded by intense emotion and imagination.

To start the flow of astral energy in the shape and direction you wish, you have to take action. Begin by having a clear picture of the result you want. You must intensely want to gain this result; if it is only a half-hearted desire, you can be sure it will not be strong enough to materialize.

As was discussed earlier, thoughtforms are created by the mind and will of a person. Even if they live for only a short time, these thoughts are actual things. They have a definite shape and color and can be seen by psychics. Each thoughtform we subconsciously or deliberately build affects our actions and environment. Every single strong thoughtform will reproduce itself in the physical world, even though it may take time. A weak thoughtform will disintegrate before anything manifests. A clear thought repeated more than once has a better chance of manifestation than a thought sent out just one time.

Since other people, particularly magicians, can torpedo your magickal efforts through negativity and jealousy before they manifest, you need to keep quiet about your activities until you see results. What you build can be destroyed.

When working magick for a desired conclusion, be sure you have considered all possible outcomes. Think over the smallest details, seeing how everything might react with some other part of your plan. If you overlook any aspect in consideration, it might pop up later and derail the whole thing.

Use gems, stones, herbs, candles, etc. to bring extra power into focus for magick. These aids will amplify whatever mood you are experiencing at the time of the working. This is one of the reasons magicians working only on the physical level use these tools.

Another helpful physical device that can also be used on the astral is the pyramid. Put a hollow cardboard or wooden pyramid in your physical ritual area to help you in gaining your desires. Align one of the flat sides to the north. Write on a piece of paper several things you would like to have happen. Place this paper under your pyramid. When you do spellwork on one of those desires, end by directing the energy into the pyramid. Create its duplicate in your astral ritual area to strengthen the magickal power.

Hard as it may sound, don't be jealous of the good fortune of another, even if that person is one of your enemies. By raising your thoughts into a positive mode, you can charge your aura with their good luck, thus improving your own future.

Astral Magick V

A good magician working in her/his astral magickal temple will be able to do powerful magickal rituals for good health, prosperity, justice, success, divination, spiritual growth, and happiness. These things will manifest in the physical. (The subject of protection will be covered in the next chapter.)

Do all your mental homework before undertaking any astral magick. Know precisely and exactly what you want to happen and why you want it to happen. Once you reach your astral magickal temple, set up your ritual area with everything you will need. As in physical magick, you can't go running out after something you forgot.

Use the following rituals in your magickal temple after you have traveled there astrally. It will be best, at first, to follow each little ritual as it is given. Later, when you are more experienced, you can change any words or create your own specific rituals for each need. Don't be surprised if one or more of your teacher-guides take part in these rituals.

If you are familiar with Wicca or ceremonial magick, cast a circle and light the directional candles. If you aren't familiar with these procedures, ask your teachers to perform this part of the ritual while you watch. The following rituals can be performed for yourself or another person.

Ritual for Good Health

Put the following items on your astral altar: a blue bag with a drawstring or some means of fastening it closed; a bowl containing feverfew, hops, mint; a blue candle; several pieces of jasper and jet.

Place the candle in the center of the altar with the pieces of jasper and jet in a circle around it. Set aside one piece of jasper and jet. Put the blue bag and the bowl of herbs between you and the candle, just outside the circle of stones.

Light the candle. Stare at the flame while visualizing the person for whom the ritual is performed as healthy and whole. Hold this visualization as long as you can.

Take up your wand and circle the bag and bowl of herbs three times sunwise. As you circle, chant:

Health to (name).

Carefully tip the herbs into the bag and add the two stones you set aside.

Using the wand or your hands, gather as much astral energy as you can. Shape it lovingly until it is a compact ball of pulsating light. Put this in the bag with the other ingredients. Fasten the bag shut.

If the bag is for another person, call the person's astral form into your sacred area and press the bag against her/his heart area until it is absorbed into the astral body. If the bag is for you, do the same on your own astral form. If the astral form won't absorb the healing bag, try to determine if the person really wants help. If the person does, but the bag refuses to go into the astral form, open it once more and add a piece of holly for protection against ill-wishing and negative thoughtforms and entities. Try again. The bag should be readily absorbed unless the person in question has a strong aversion to being healed.

Close the magickal circle and sit for a few moments in positive vibrations with your teacher-guides.

Ritual for Prosperity

Put the following items on your astral altar: two gold and two silver coins; a bowl containing chamomile, Irish moss, and vervain; a piece each of ruby, peridot, turquoise, and tiger's eye; a green bag with a button or snap closure.

Stir the herbs in the bowl with your wand while chanting:

> *Powerful herbs, bring wealth to me.*
> *As I will, so shall it be.*

Pour the herbs into the bag. Gather astral energy with your hands; form it into a little ball and put it in the bag with the herbs.

Tap each stone with the wand and chant:

> *Like to like, the power of these stones attracts.*

Either place them in the bag or set them aside to be made into a necklace. Close the bag and press it into the throat center area of your astral form.

Tap each coin and say:

> *Silver and gold, silver and gold,*
> *Bring me all my life can hold.*

String the coins on a chain to make a necklace; the stones can be added to these. Or you can create earrings out of the coins.

Hold your arms over your head as if you were making a funnel into your astral form. Visualize prosperity in all the forms in which you want it to appear in your life. See and feel these prosperous manifestations pouring down between your arms into your crown chakra. Accept them and absorb them.

Ritual for Success

For this ritual you should have a definite goal in mind, not success in general: getting a new job, selling a house or property, buying a specific house or property, opening a business, passing a test.

Put the following items on your astral altar: a bowl of mugwort, rose, hawthorn, and mint; a wide copper bracelet set with crystals; a green or light brown candle.

Set the candle in the center of your astral altar and light it. Tap the bowl of herbs five times with your wand and burn the herbs in your incense burner. Stare into the candle flame while you visualize the success happening that you want to happen. Take as much time as necessary to do this.

Pick up the copper bracelet with the tip of your wand. See and feel the astral energy gathering on the bracelet. Carry it in this fashion around the ritual area while you say:

> Cosmic power, come to me.
> Successful is what I will to be.

When you get back to your place at the altar, take the bracelet off the wand and rub the astral energy into the band. As you do this, continue to see yourself as successful in your proposed endeavor. Place the bracelet on the wrist of your power hand (the one you use to write).

Ritual for Divination

This brief ritual can be used for any astral divination or to gain powers in divination. Put the following items on your astral altar: a goblet of white wine; your tarot cards, runes, whatever you plan to use; a large unpolished crystal; incense containing mugwort; two silver candles.

Place one lighted candle on each side of your altar with the divination tools between them. Set the goblet of wine nearby. Sprinkle a little incense into the incense burner.

Take the crystal into both hands and hold it high. Watch the astral energy collect around it. Then press the crystal gently to your third eye in the center of your forehead. Feel the collected energy being absorbed into this light center and activating your psychic talents. When the energy has been completely absorbed by your astral body, set the crystal back on the altar to collect more energy.

Circle the divinatory tools three times sunwise with your wand, while saying:

Grant me the power of foretelling.

Lift the goblet in a salute and then take a sip:

One for magick.

Take another sip:

One for power.

Take a third sip:

One for "seeing" in this hour.

Put the goblet back on the altar and lay out the cards, cast the runes, whatever. Carefully note the layout and write it down when you return from your astral journey.

Ritual for Spiritual Growth

Put the following items on your astral altar: three gold candles; a small golden statue of a phoenix; three yellow diamonds; a bowl of laurel leaves, marigold, and St. John's wort.

Position the three candles in a triangle, with one making the point away from where you stand at your altar. Light them and place a yellow diamond beside each one of them. Put the phoenix statue in the center of this triangle.

Burn the herbs in the incense burner. Sit in a chair close to the altar where you can easily see the lighted candles and the phoenix statue. See the glow from the candles expand until the entire ritual area is bathed in a golden light.

While you breathe in this golden light, chant:

> *O golden powers of energy,*
> *O astral powers, wondrous fair,*
> *Hear my words of trust and grace,*
> *Winging through the astral air.*
> *Illuminate deep Mysteries,*
> *Bring me insight into fate.*
> *Fill my life with truth and joy,*
> *Spiritual illumination great.*

Pay close attention to anything you hear or see while you sit contemplating the golden light. You may even be whirled away to meet a new teacher, take part in a ceremony, or experience an initiation. If none of these events happen immediately, don't assume you have failed. You may experience them during an astral-dream, or you may go through a time of physical preparation and undergo them at a later time.

Ritual for Happiness and Love

Absolutely do not use this ritual to try to make someone love you! In fact, never use any spellworking or ritual to force someone to love you. Avoid the negative karma you will have to pay for controlling another person.

Put the following items on your astral altar: two pink candles, one with your name carved on it, the other with "my true love" carved into it; a vase of beautiful pink roses; a bottle of rose or apple blossom oil; a small bell.

Place a pink candle on each side of the vase of roses, but don't light them. Lightly anoint your heart light center with the perfumed oil.

Ring the bell three times and call upon the deities of love to bless you with their presence. Wait patiently for their arrival. They will appear in your ritual space as great glowing forms of flashing pink and golden light. The vibrations coming from them will be of unconditional love and comfort.

Explain to these deities in your own words why you want a true and loving companion in your life. If they ask you questions, and they well might, answer as truthfully as you can. When this talk is over, the deities will light the candles for you with their great, all-reaching power. A single pink rose will rise from the vase and hang in the air over the altar. Swirls of pink and golden light will gather around this rose, gradually making it into an almost transparent form.

A shaft of light suddenly goes from the rose to your heart center. You feel a slight tugging as your true feelings toward love and companionship are poured out from your astral form and into the rose. The rose becomes a ball of astral energy and light and disappears. It has gone to be manifested in the physical.

The great deities fill your ritual space with sensations of love and then disappear. Ring the bell three times again and thank them for their aid.

Ritual for Justice

Put the following items on your astral altar: two deep purple candles; a curl of unicorn hair; a vase of carnation flowers; a four-leaf clover; a silver headband set with a center stone of dark amethyst.

Set the candles on the altar, one on each side, and light them. Position the flowers between the candles, with the headband, clover, and unicorn hair nearby. Sprinkle cedar incense into your burner.

Clearly state to the great astral powers what your need is for justice. Listen to any words which may come back to you. If you are at fault, do not finish this ritual. If you are partially at fault, resolve to change your part before continuing. Be truthful!

Gather a small ball of astral energy, and mold it into a compact ball. Hold the clover and the unicorn hair to this ball until they are absorbed. Swallow the ball of energy.

Be very certain you want to continue with this ritual before you put on the headband. Position the amethyst in the headband so that it lies over the center of your forehead.

Chant:

> *Great Ones, come and join with me*
> *And the Justice Deities.*
> *Change my luck. Make me bold.*
> *Bring me wealth and love to hold,*
> *Accomplishments and friendships true.*
> *For this aid, I do thank You.*

Now close your eyes and stare upward, as if looking at the inside of the center of your forehead. (If this is done even in the physical body, you will eventually see an eye looking back at you.) Look into this eye until it dissolves into a series of pictures. These pictures will give you clues as to what you should and should not do in your quest for justice. Unless you are responsible for part of the problem, it is unlikely you will be required to do anything other than let the greater astral powers take care of the problem.

Changing Future Events

We have more control over and more possibility of changing individual future karma than we have of affecting group karma, such as that of a nation or the world as a whole. This is because there are fewer people involved in individual karma than national or world karma. Every human has free will to create or not create, to do or not do, what is best for them. Anyone who has given readings on the future, using the tarot or other methods, knows that the more people involved in a particular future event, the more likely it is to change suddenly. Therefore, if you see a national event where the vast majority of people involved are absolutely determined on a course of action, you will not be likely to make any changes.

Individual futures are in a more flexible state than the futures of nations or of the world. Even in individual future events which seem to already be inflexible, the magician can make small changes. The wisdom lies in learning where to put the pressure. A tiny bit of pressure applied to a specific part of an upcoming individual event may be enough to create a totally different outcome.

Astral Magick VI

Changing or shaping a future event to better suit your desires is important to almost everyone, unless you have a martyr complex and love to live in negative circumstances.

Suppose there is an event, such as a job interview or confrontation with an unpleasant person, coming up in the near future. You have the feeling that things may not go well for you or end in your favor. You have to be careful here that you are not thinking about controlling someone or making the person act against her/his nature, but are planning only to put a little pressure in specific areas to produce a more positive outcome.

No matter what any psychic has told you or what you intuitively believe will happen, if a situation is negative, try to make small changes in the future event. Never be a martyr to circumstances if you can at all help it! And you can always "help it," to some degree.

If the future event is a job interview, for example, and you think you might be up against unfair competition or not be given a fair hearing, do some astral magick to even things up. Make an astral visit to the prospective employer and concisely tell her/him all the reasons you should have the job and why you would make a better employee than the competition. Listen to any answers you get back. With a little astral discussion you may find out you wouldn't like the employer or the business in which you are asking for work. Then again, you may discover opportunities and benefits you didn't know existed. Don't try to force the employer to accept you. Simply present your case, just as you would if you were granted a special interview in person. Then thank the employer and leave.

Confrontations with people you would rather not see or talk to are difficult in the best of times. However, there are a number of astral ways to help with the problem. At one time, I had to face a person who had caused me great pain and had a nasty habit of intimidating every woman he was around. I knew that bringing up old issues would never get him to admit he had been wrong or apologize, so I determined that all I wanted was to conduct present business in at least a neutral atmosphere. While out on the astral, I created a huge cannon. I armed it with an inexhaustible supply of sticky pink cannonballs and began shooting them at the man. I drowned him in the color pink. All the way to the meeting I kept that cannon going. The business was conducted in a civilized manner. The man was very polite (an unheard-of occurrence) and seemed in a daze when I left. Use your creative visualization in any positive way you can.

If you get strong intuitive feelings about a proposed trip, for example, you can astral travel to see what the problems might be. If the problems are major (auto or plane crashes), revise your schedule to take a different flight or another route. If there is a possible assault or burglary, change as many of the circumstances as you can: avoid a specific street, restaurant, or hotel; don't accept the room number you saw; get a burglar alarm; wear a protective amulet; cleanse your home or car and set up astral Watchers. Never accept that you can't change the future to some degree, at least!

A friend had an astral vision about her death in a car jacking. She decided she had too many things to do to be bothered with an exit from the physical at that time. So she began with making out a will (something she had avoided doing), then changed her travel plans, made sure she drove with all the doors locked, and for added insurance took a self-defense course. The car jacking was attempted, but with the doors locked the perpetrators couldn't get in. One of the men was later apprehended by the police because my friend deliberately ran over his foot and broke it.

Remember what was said about karma? Never accept that it can't be changed, and be willing to make all the changes you can. If this sounds like a lot of work, it is. But it's your life, so why not try to make it safe and pleasant?

Twelve

Defense Against the Dark Side

If you have been told, or have talked yourself into believing, that there is no dark side to magick, that no one can affect you through their magickal efforts or negative thoughts, then you had better prepare yourself for problems. I'm not speaking of Satanism; Satanism is a religion perverted from Christianity. Dark magick and ill-wishing have nothing to do with religion. Any person can wish you ill; remember, thoughts are things and have power. Any magician who is jealous, feels threatened, or thinks you are impeding her/his progress can, and might, cast a spell (small or large) against you.

Anyone practicing magick will sooner or later draw the attention of envious people and unscrupulous dark magicians, out of jealousy if nothing else. However, knowing that

185

such negative practices and magicians exist doesn't mean you have to go around with a paranoid attitude. All you need to do is use common sense, take sensible precautions, and stay alert.

Sometimes the problems arise from personal interactions. You just don't like a particular person and she/he is hateful to you, all for no apparent reason. You can bet the roots of these problems are in the past somewhere. Perhaps in your past life or lives you were not directly involved with the troublesome person, but she/he was somewhere in the periphery of your activities. Knowing your past lives, or at least how to check into them, can be valuable when trying to understand present conflicts and antagonisms with other people.

Scientists have studied the effects of blessing and cursing on plants and found them to work. Distance makes no difference in the results. Of course, distance would make no difference since the desired effect, deliberately or subconsciously, is shaped on the astral, sent through the astral to its destination, and then manifested. Some magicians don't need to have a piece of your clothing, a lock of hair, or even a letter hand-written by you to zero in on your vibrations and cause problems.

However, most magicians and astral travelers are not in much danger from their fellow human creatures. The greatest dangers don't come from other humans, but from negative astral entities who resent your progress in astral magick and healing.

Since being on the astral planes heightens the awareness of all your senses, negative forces can be identified at once. Repeated astral journeying will heighten your awareness both while you are in the astral and after you return to the physical body.

Because you can contact any person from history while on the astral, you can have access to precise knowledge of self-defense and protection. Just call upon powerful past magicians whose ethics and ideas match yours. I strongly suggest that you do not call upon questionable magicians out of the past. Those who were borderline or downright negative in their practices will contaminate your aura and often influence you in ways you won't want.

Astral Enemies

On occasion you will run the risk of encountering a powerful negative entity on the astral. If you have worked in the occult field for some time, you can bet that sooner or later you will make enemies, both in the astral and in the physical. Keeping quiet about your magickal work helps you avoid physical enemies, who usually attack through jealousy and envy. Astral enemies can't be distracted in this way, but remaining confident and calm will enable you to repulse their attacks, whether in the astral or in the physical.

Psychic attacks, whether initiated by physical humans or astral beings, can be difficult to detect. We are trained to be "sensible" and therefore to discount unpleasant happenings as chance. Don't be paranoid, but realize that too many negative happenings mean you are under attack. For instance, if you have a long run of bad luck, flat tires, small accidents, illnesses, and clumsiness that is totally unlike you, then you had better seriously start protecting yourself.

Everyone who works on the astral planes learns that there are undesirable, often dangerous, entities living there. Dwellers on the astral include the astral forms of once-living humans, human-created thoughtforms, and astral entities who were never in human form. As in meeting strangers on this plane of existence, we must be aware and wary when meeting astral entities. Sometimes we are subjected to these entities through the habits of someone close to us. Alcoholics, drug addicts, and constantly negative people drag undesirable entities around with them all the time.

Whether the attacks come directly from astral entities or from another magician using the negative forces of astral entities, the methods of protection are basically the same. The magician cleans her/his aura, sets up specific protection measures, and sends back the negative energy.

Both Max Freedom Long, who wrote about the kahunas of Hawaii, and Arthur Guirdham believed that some mental illnesses were caused by the invasion of spirits, rather like a haunting.

Actually, most people are very resistant to invading entities, even those entities sent by powerful magicians. The people who seem to be affected are those who have deep guilt feelings about present or past lives. This type of astral attack through possession is extremely rare.

Astral Defense I

Fighting back against attack through the astral is something every magician, whether working on the astral or not, should know about. It doesn't matter whether the attacking force has been generated by a physical being or is living in the astral, the defense is basically the same.

The magician must begin by repairing her/his light centers and aura before astral traveling. If feelings of guilt or regret still linger, although you have done what is possible to correct any imbalance, do a special meditation with the express purpose of dropping these negative feelings down the well.

Call upon your teacher-guides and the Watcher before you project onto the astral planes. You want to be totally protected while you journey to your astral ritual area.

Once in your temple, place a goblet of spring water, a small plate of salt, a lighted white candle, a small jar of frankincense, and a bell on your altar. At least two of your teachers will help you with this ritual. It cannot be emphasized enough, that everything you do on the astral *must* be real to you. You must be able to sense with all your five senses for astral magick to be powerful.

Using the blade of your dagger, put three portions of salt into the chalice of water. Stir the water three times sunwise with the dagger.

One of the teachers will carry the incense burner and put on the frankincense as needed. The other will carry the bell and white candle.

Carrying the chalice of water, sprinkle drops around the edges of the entire room. Behind you comes the teacher swinging the smoking incense burner and the other teacher carrying the candle and ringing the bell. Sprinkle around every single room, closet, and hall in your temple.

Return to your altar and replace the chalice, candle, incense burner, and bell. With your ritual sword, draw a triangle of light on the other side of the altar from where you will stand. This is a safety enclosure to imprison negative thoughtforms and astral creatures.

Move back to your regular place at the altar and hold the sword upright before you. The teachers will stand on either side of you with their swords ready. Challenge your attackers to show themselves within the triangle.

Astral creatures must appear if challenged. Thoughtforms built by physical humans will try to avoid this confrontation, but eventually must appear if you keep repeating the challenge. When these creatures are standing across the altar from you, demand that they name themselves. There will likely ensue a battle of wills, but if you hold firm, these creatures must name themselves, who sent them, and their purpose.

The next step will determine your character as a magician. If these beings are from the astral, call upon the astral police to remove and confine them to the lower levels. Keep these astral creatures away from you by keeping your ritual sword pointed at them. Your teachers will help.

If, however, they are thoughtforms created by another human, you must decide whether their sending was subconscious or deliberate. If they were subconsciously created, find out what emotions and events caused this. You may be surprised to find that their creator is someone very close to you. Some of them may even be your own creations. Obviously, you don't want to hurt yourself or someone who is not deliberately causing you this trouble. With your teachers' help, you must now change the vibrations of these thoughtforms from negative to positive and return them to their creators. It may take much time and energy to completely transform these creatures.

If the thoughtforms have been deliberately sent, you must decide if you are willing to make the effort to return them as they are and watch the negativity that will occur upon their return. I don't believe in being a doormat and have no guilty feelings about returning these negatives to the person or persons who made them.

Never specify what you want to happen to the sender. This will lock you into sharing their troubles. In fact, it is better not even to suggest that these thoughtforms return to a particular person. Just return them to their maker; they will know the right way home.

A battle will probably take place at this time. Follow your teachers' lead and use your sword to keep these negative thoughtforms away from you. Deliberately created thoughtforms are much more aggressive than those subconsciously formed. Drive them out by seeing a great stream of white light coming from the sword tip. Aim it at the forms within the triangle until they fade away into nothing.

Lay aside your ritual sword and disrobe. Let your teachers clothe you in flexible blue astral armor that will remain on your astral form even after you are back in the physical body. This astral armor will help prevent attack through your light centers.

Take extra care to call upon your teachers and the Watcher each time you journey into the astral for a time after this.

If you encounter a negative entity or thoughtform while in the astral and cannot get to the safety of your ritual temple or teachers, stand your ground. Face the entity and don't let its projected emotion of fear rattle you; these types of entities gain extra strength by attacking you first with fear, which may cause you in turn to project fear by being afraid. These entities feed and grow on fear. Instead, shout at them! Both thoughts and vocalized sound, even on the astral, create vibrations. A shout produces vibrations strong enough to forcefully carry the entities away from you, rather like a tidal wave.

Uninvited Astral Entities

On rare occasions, you may find yourself half in, half out of your physical body and unable to move. Usually this is no cause for alarm. Simply complete the withdrawal of the astral body or reseat it in the physical. On even rarer occasions, however, you may find yourself in such a position being threatened by a negative astral entity.

When this happened to me, I was totally unprepared. I knew little about astral travel and even less about astral entities. However, there was never a doubt in my mind about the kind of creature that faced me. My soon-to-be ex-spouse and I had just had a terrible row over him coming in drunk again and knocking me about. As I lay asleep, I became aware that what I called "me" was half out of my physical body. The dark room was suddenly filled with a bright glow, and in the doorway to the bedroom stood a being. I don't remember what it looked like, but the evil coming from it couldn't be mistaken.

My consciousness was working perfectly; I knew if I could move some part of my physical body the danger would be over. Then began the hardest work I ever did, holding off that entity with one part of my mind, while another part literally forced one of my fingers to move. I was shaking when my astral body slid back into place. The entity no longer threatened. I remember sitting up in bed, thinking to myself, "You bastard! How dare you bring that home with you!" I jumped when I felt a hand on my shoulder and heard a voice in my head saying, "If you don't like what's happening, don't stay. It's your choice." It was my teacher-guardian making himself known. I made my plans and got myself and my children out of the situation.

If I had known more about magick at that time, I could have made an astral dome of protection or constructed a Watcher thoughtform (different from the Watcher at the gate) to warn me of such things. Of course, these things wouldn't have corrected the relationship or solved the problem of negative entities getting a free ride into my environment. My teacher was right; the choice was mine to stay and see more of "those things" by keeping bad company.

Astrally constructing a dome of protection only works if you do not have the perpetrator or company-keeper of the negative entities within the dome with you. If you can get this person out, a dome is an excellent way to protect yourself, your family, pets, property, vehicles, and place of business.

Just as an actual physical fence or wall will not protect your property from gophers and other rodents, the astral protective dome will not protect you from the two-legged kind of troublemakers who enter your home, bringing their unwelcome company with them. The only way you have of protecting yourself against these people and their unseen travelers is to stay away from them. To do this may mean severing relationships and friendships. You have to decide what your personal responsibility is.

Astral Defense II

Building a dome of protection isn't difficult; it involves concentrated visualization, though. You can either make the dome like a hemisphere or like a geodesic structure covering everything. Begin by going onto the astral planes where you can see all energy forms. Detect which ones are negative; call upon your teachers for help and, with your ritual sword (it will appear in your hand as soon as you think of it), run the negative entities completely beyond the actual physical boundaries of your property. Your teachers will stand guard against their return while you complete the construction of the dome.

Beginning at the foundation of this structure, piece by piece visualize the dome taking shape. Make its foundation conform to your property boundaries, then take the dome-shape as it rises upward. Build the dome carefully and with great energy, taking as long as necessary.

When the dome completely covers everything, you can reinforce it with another magickal visualization. See this dome sprayed with a silvery reflective coating, then covered with blinding white light. The dome itself will deter entry by negative thoughtforms, unless they are physically given a ride inside by a human. The reflective coating will send attacking thoughtforms straight back to the senders. The white light will transform any weak negative thoughtforms (from inside or outside) into positive energy and store it for use.

Astral Personalities

It makes no difference whether you are speaking of the physical or the astral plane, when a group of beings get together there automatically begins a round of activity within all the auras. There is a jockeying for dominance. If you are aware of this, you can avoid being bullied into a subservient position by another.

Both astral beings and humans journeying on the astral planes have visible auras. When two auras come in contact, information about the two entities is instantly passed back and forth. Keep your intuitive senses alert while you are out on the astral. They will be your first warning if something is wrong or dangerous.

If you encounter such an astral situation, immediately call upon the white light to surround you. This is often enough to make the offending entity uncomfortable and leave. If it still persists in annoying or threatening you, yell for your teacher-guides. There is strength in numbers. Ordinarily, this is quite enough to make the entity give up and go away.

Astral Defense III

Defending yourself in the astral isn't much different from defending yourself in the physical. There are certain defensive exercises (the mental equivalent of physical judo) that, practiced in small doses, will come into play automatically when you need defense against bigger dangers.

The first line of defense should be the circle or, as some call it, a ring-pass-not. This is the simple practice of visualizing yourself completely surrounded by a ring of white fire. This ring will go with you whenever you move, so you don't have to worry about losing it if you need to get away from a particular astral area. You can mentally "draw" the circle with the forefinger of your power hand. I prefer to call my astral ritual sword for the job; it teleports instantly from my astral magickal temple to my hand. Then, beginning right in front of me, I draw the flame-circle with the sword, going sunwise. I make the circle very strong by drawing that line three times, overlapping the ends. When finished, I stand the sword directly before me, right on the beginning and ending point of the circle. No astral entity or thought-form can cross this flame-circle unless you let it in.

I have found this same protection technique to be very effective in the physical when I am driving my car. The flame-circle seems to repel incoming hostilities from other drivers and negative vibrations that could attract accidents, and to dissipate the confusion so common when traveling in strange places.

Perhaps the annoying astral entity won't give you time to draw your flame-circle. Take quick action by calling up a potent ball of blue-white light; surround yourself with it instantly. Then gather more balls of this light and hurl them at the solar plexus center of the offending entity. This causes a scrambling of any emotional hook-up it is attempting with you. Keep throwing the balls of light until the entity is thoroughly confused and retreats. This works whether the astral being is an astral entity, an astral projection of another person, or a thoughtform.

If you suspect that the offending entity is an astral projection of another person, also "blind" it by throwing balls of light directly at the center of the being's forehead where the third eye is. This psychic eye is the "seeing" mechanism used while in the astral body. Splashing concentrated white light into this center temporarily keeps your attacker from being able to "see" where you go or what you do next.

It is a good idea to wear a physical protective amulet or piece of jewelry, or even a stone, which makes you feel protected. When you are out and about on the astral, feel the astral equivalent of your protective charm on your astral body. Touch it; see it; know that it is there. This charm, along with your astral aura, will be your first line of warning of approaching danger and your first line of defense, if the danger approaches unnoticed.

An amulet or stone can be deliberately charged to perform protective duties. Stones naturally have certain vibrations of protection, healing, power in magickal spells, etc. Don't try to put protective vibrations onto a healing stone, for example. This will only confuse the vibrations, and you will end up with a stone that is useless until your added-on vibrations fade away.

To determine the natural vibrations of a stone, hold it in your power hand, close your eyes, and concentrate on the feelings you receive from it. If you have difficulty deciding on what the vibrations imply, hold the stone to your third eye or against your solar plexus. This should clear up the information.

Occasionally, you will pick up a stone that is "confused." It has either been handled by so many people that its natural vibrations are totally mixed up with all the emotions of its handlers, or the atmosphere of the store (or wherever it is being traded or sold) is so permeated with a particular vibration that the stone has absorbed this strong emotion on top of its natural inclination.

If you feel really drawn to the stone, take it home and do a cleansing. First, wash it in cold running water and dry it carefully. Then bury it for three days in a container of salt. Throw the salt away, as it will soak up impurities and negative vibrations, making it unsafe to use for anything else. Wash and dry the stone again. Put it in a place where it will not be handled by anyone for several days before again trying to read its true vibrations.

If the stone is in any setting except high-quality gold, don't subject it to the salt burial. This may well corrode or pit the setting. Instead, dissolve three tablespoons of salt in a cup of water. Thoroughly dip the jewelry into the salt-water mixture, then immediately wash it again under cold running water and dry. I have found that a few minutes in one of the vibrating jewelry cleaners does an exceptional job of removing unwanted vibrations. I don't know if this is from the physical vibrations of the cleaner or the electricity from the motor, but it works!

If an entity should actually get hold of your astral body, immediately and violently chop down on the offending appendage while seeing your whole body as living white fire. Kick out sharply with your foot to the knee or groin area (root center, remember?). Smack the heel of your hand into the third eye (brow center). Punch the solar plexus.

While you are defending yourself by using your astral body just as you would your physical, don't overlook the power of the astral "voice." Shout "Be gone!" or "Back off!" with great indignation that anyone or anything should have the temerity to lay hands on you.

Develop an attitude of "don't you dare bother or threaten me!" when traveling in the astral. Astral entities, like physical attackers, usually prey on those they feel are afraid or timid.

Generally, having this attitude is enough to keep all but the very determined negative entities from annoying you at all. They may hang around the fringes of your sight as you move through the astral, but they are usually too cowardly and hesitant to actually attack a confident astral traveler.

Making a guardian thoughtform in the shape of a ball of white light is always a useful warning device. Mold the thought-form out of astral energy and set it on your shoulder with instructions to notify you at once of the approach of any negative entities during your journey.

You can also create such a guardian and put it on your physical shoulder when you have to walk through potentially dangerous areas. Instruct it to warn you of potential dangers and to help in your defense if necessary.

A friend had to walk through a dim parking lot at the end of each work day. Alice created such a guardian thoughtform and set it on her physical shoulder each evening before she went to her car. One winter evening she was suddenly faced with a young mugger who had been hiding behind the cars. When he ordered her to give him her purse, Alice reached up, patted her guardian, and calmly said, "Get him!" The young man's eyes went wide, and he ran the other way as if demons were after him.

Never consider yourself defenseless when out on the astral. You can always defend yourself from astral "muggers" and other undesirables. And remember, always yell for your teacher-guides while you are doing the primary things to protect yourself. They can be there at a moment's notice.

Astral Magickal Laws

One of the most controversial rules in magick is: Never tell others what you are doing in magick unless they are in total agreement with you. This not only dissipates the energy if they are not in agreement with you, but also gives opponents the opportunity to undo your magickal efforts. Some magicians don't believe that talking about their magickal work does any harm. However, I can tell you from personal experience that the majority of people (especially non-magicians) will overload you with at least sub-conscious negative thoughtforms every time.

When working on the astral, you will find that there is no longer any slowness of the physical body to contend with. Actions happen as soon as you think of them. Keep the intellect out of it. Don't give up common sense and ethics, but when in the astral for whatever reason, let your emotional body respond. The intellect's habit of analyzing everything to the point of distraction only confuses the issue and makes it harder for you to take action and do your work.

The power of thoughts exists in greater strength in the astral than in the physical, so watch your thoughts. Thoughts while in the physical body radiate outward like a stone dropped in water; their power continues to exist as long as you hold the thought. When you cease to think that thought or change your thoughts, the radiation of the original thought disappears. While in the astral, the radiation of thoughts is even more powerful. However, the vibrational activity of thought is still the same. Hold true to your magickal thoughts until you can feel the manifestation come alive.

Since threads run from one auric shield to another through thoughts or spells sent, you must take great care to sever that thread before you leave your astral magickal area. By allowing the connecting threads to remain, this will not release the magickal powers to manifest. Thinking constantly about your magickal work will reconnect the threads also.

You should also look for connecting auric threads before you do any magick on the physical or the astral. A few magicians are unscrupulous enough to sneak in a connecting thread so they can syphon off your magickal energy for their own use. The most common threat, however, doesn't come from another magician. It comes from non-magickal people who subconsciously tune in on your increased energy flow during magickal procedures. Like the psychic vampires I talked about earlier, who use your physical presence to get at your physical energy, these people are vampires on the astral levels.

The only way to sever these auric threads, and keep them from reattaching, is to cut them with your astral ritual sword. If you feel threads attached, or find one attached, and can't go into the astral to fight them, close your eyes for a few moments. Visualize your aura and see where the threads are; they are usually connected directly to a light center. Connection to the solar plexus is the most common.

Relax and see yourself with your ritual sword in one hand. See the sword turning to a glowing white-hot. Don't try to saw the threads, but rather burn them in two with one swift stroke. As soon as the threads are loose, immediately clothe yourself in your protective astral armor.

Now that you are protected once more, demand to know who has sent these threads. You should be able to follow each thread back to its source and either get a clear picture of the person responsible or at least have an intuitive feeling about the sender. Decide what actions you need to take, physically or astrally, to eliminate this problem.

Detecting Possible Future Events

Events of a strong emotional nature seem to cast a kind of shadow ahead of their occurrence. This often gives us the feeling of waiting for the other shoe to drop. If you are used to working in the astral and your psychic senses are finely tuned from being used, you will get adequate warning to deflect these totally, or at least in part. The hardest part is being impartial enough to truthfully see what is programmed to possibly happen in your future.

We have been told for so long that we can do nothing but accept what will happen, that we often find ourselves in an emotional dilemma. Do you accept whatever comes because it might be karmic, or are you worthy of better things because you have made an effort to change your spiritual life? Here, the magician must know her/his own worth without getting carried away, while at the same time being willing to experience certain negative events because these events promote spiritual growth. Personally, I feel I am quite capable of learning lessons without being dragged to the depths of despair.

The more determined people are involved in a future event, the less flexible that event will be to change. This doesn't mean you shouldn't try to change small things within that event. Even little changes can help.

Astral Defense V

If you are plagued by a feeling of "impending doom," make an astral journey to your magickal temple. Call upon your teachers for help and protection. As soon as they arrive within your ritual space, begin gazing into the future through your crystal ball. Try to determine exactly what upcoming event is causing this feeling of uneasiness. The more emotional this event will be, and the more personal impact it will have upon you directly, the harder it will be for you to have a detached perspective in viewing it. It is possible that you won't see all of the future event in any one crystal gazing. Knowing how we react emotionally, the subconscious mind often gives us unpleasant information in bits and pieces, until we can accept the total view.

After you have gotten a picture of at least part of this future unpleasant event, consider carefully what pressure you can bring to bear magickally on a small action within the event. You may have to try several of the smaller events before you can find where you are able to make a change.

Visualize this change taking place, and keep visualizing until you can make the new action stable. This takes a lot of concentration and determination. Making future changes like this is difficult.

Keep viewing the future event, selecting one smaller action at a time to change. Work thoroughly with each change until it manifests within the crystal ball. If actual physical changes in such things as plans or actions are needed, do them as soon as you can. When no more changes can be done or will hold within the crystal ball, then you will know you have done all you can about the future event. The rest of it you must accept.

The use of stones and herbs in both physical and astral magick is very important. Each type of stone and herb has its own specific vibrations. The magician must study and learn how to apply these vibrations in order to more fully empower her/his rituals and spellworkings to gain a particular manifestation. However, there are other aids which also amplify your astral magickal powers.

A mirror can be used to reflect unwanted negatives. Used as a shield in magickal work, a mirror will return to the attacker the full force of the attacking spellwork.

Dancing to build energy can build up an energy vortex upon which the magician can draw during magickal work. Dancing or turning in a sunwise direction creates positive energy, while dancing in the opposite direction creates negative energy. Sometimes it becomes necessary to send out bursts of negative energy, followed by bursts of the positive kind, to disrupt incoming energy flow during an attack.

Playing musical instruments, such as deep bass drums, cymbals, and the Egyptian sistrum, can aid the magician in her/his protective rituals. The vibrations of the sounds of these instruments seem to have a disturbing effect upon attacking thoughtforms or astral entities.

By their very nature, circles of standing stones create pools of protective power. You can create an astral ritual area within a circle of standing stones. If under attack in the astral and the integrity of your regular ritual space has been compromised, you can retreat to the circle of standing stones. This secondary ritual temple, built in nature, is also very powerful when working with elementals and the forces of nature.

Pyramids have great protective benefits, as mentioned earlier. Place a physical one in your car to deflect danger and help you avoid accidents. It doesn't have to be very big, and it can be made out of wood or even cardboard. For added protection of your astral ritual space, place a small pyramid somewhere within its perimeter.

Many other tools and aids can be valuable when having to deal with dark magickal attacks. Use your intuition, imagination, and creative faculties.

Astral Defense VI

Set aside a time to go to your astral magickal temple and create any magickal tools you have not yet prepared. If in doubt as to what you might need in the near future, talk it over with your teacher-guides. Be sure you store everything in your store rooms, neatly and correctly. Powerful tools, such as certain stones, special swords and daggers, and amulets, should be wrapped in pieces of silk and stored in individual chests or boxes.

Schedule one astral journey to your temple just to look through the ancient books in your library. If you find reference to a magician who successfully handled an astral attack, make plans to visit with that magician. Question your teachers about ancient forgotten magickal procedures. Learn all you can.

Further fortifying your astral magickal area may become necessary at some time in your magickal development. Periodic cleansing and purifying with salt, water, bell, and candle should be performed as a precaution.

After one of your regular cleansings, return to your altar and create mentally four gold seals for each window, door, and mirror in your temple. These portals are the usual entry places for thoughtforms and other snooping astral travelers. On each seal draw a pentagram or the Tyr rune (an arrow pointing upward) with your wand.

Pass each seal through the incense smoke and sprinkle it with the consecrated water-salt solution. Take the seals and place four at each portal: one on each of the sides of the window frames; one on each side of the door, one overhead, and one right in the middle of the door; one on each of the sides of the mirror frames. After you have applied all the seals on each portal, tap each seal firmly with your wand. This sets the guards into action.

When you have finished sealing every door, window, and mirror in your temple, return to the altar. Firmly give the order:

What I have sealed, no other can unseal! This magickal
temple is secured against all invaders! This is my will!

Setting Up an Astral Security System

You can set up psychic security for the protection of personal documents, belongings, your home, pets, family, yourself, or your business. Build a wall of energy around the people and places you want protected. Then surround this wall with an area of deliberate confusion. Usually this is enough to deter any astral entity or traveler from breaking in and causing problems. As an added precaution, place warning thoughtform guards in this layer of confusion; they should be programmed to notify you of any intruders. If properly done, this method is better than burglar alarms and watchdogs.

Setting up Watchers will only be effective if you also have built an astral dome of protection. The Watchers are just that: Watchers and alarms. If you keep your intuitive senses alert, you will be able to pick up their warnings any time a negative astral entity or thoughtform invades, or attempts to invade, your environment.

Specialized Watchers can also be created specifically for guarding important documents. It is possible that someone might be stupid enough to try to physically steal these documents. But with more people learning how to astral travel to prearranged destinations, it is more likely that the theft will be of the ideas and not the actual document itself. This scenario can cover anything from business plans and projected purchases, rival bids on jobs or property, to ideas you may be planning to present to your boss or a prospective customer, thereby gaining a raise in salary or position. It never pays to be lax in protecting yourself in these areas.

You can also create a personalized Watcher, a thoughtform that stays right with you and is set to give you an alarm any time you are physically in danger. These are especially valuable with the crime rate soaring as it is.

Astral Defense VII

Creating a Watcher thoughtform can be done in either the physical or the astral. The procedure is done exactly the same way in both planes. First, determine exactly what simple set of instructions will be programmed into the Watcher. Don't make the instructions too difficult or complicated as a Watcher responds best when things are simple.

When you have the instructions simplified, down to a sentence of orders, go to a place where you won't be disturbed. Begin forming astral energy with your hands. Keep at this until you have a ball of compact energy about the size and shape of a basketball. When working in the astral, you will be able to both see and feel this energy thoughtform. If working in the physical, you can tell you have the energy between your hands by the tingling feeling and sensation of warmth.

Hold the ball of energy to your lips and breathe life into it. Then hold it to your third eye and mentally transfer to the Watcher the exact instructions you want it to follow. If you are setting these Watchers into the layer of confusion about your dome of protection, project "Protect all this property and all the people and pets who live here." Then gently toss it into the air and order it to take its position of defense.

A Watcher programmed to guard documents should be programmed with the instructions, then set in the room where these documents are. It will confuse and repel any astral intruder who attempts to enter and read the documents.

Personal, individualized Watchers can be programmed to protect your vehicle. Their form should naturally be placed within the truck, car, van, etc.

The Watcher you create to guard yourself should be placed on top of your head, right over the crown light center. At first, this personal Watcher may take some getting used to. Its energy may make your hair feel as if something is crawling around in it, or you may have trouble with static electricity. If this becomes a problem, you may want to coat the Watcher with a static-reducing finish.

Each Watcher will send the kind of alarm that has the best chance of alerting its creator. You may suddenly become uneasy, feel you are being watched, or wake out of a sound sleep to see astral fireworks going on. If you give your Watcher permission to repel attack in whatever way it sees as best, it will automatically take defensive action upon any signs of attempted astral invasion. You can program the Watcher to allow the entrance of friends who visit you astrally.

If you are thinking about doing any unwelcome astral snooping on your own, consider what a burst of energy from a Watcher will do to your aura. This astral defense system is nearly impossible to circumvent or disconnect. Watchers respond only to the instructions of their creators.

You have every right to defend yourself, your family and pets, your property and ideas. No one has any right whatsoever to invade your personal space uninvited during astral travel. The intent of the astral invasion may only be for snooping purposes, but consider that gossip about your private affairs can do as much damage as an outright attack on your person. Don't allow it!

Thirteen

No Broom Required

You now know that astral projection and travel is not difficult to do, and you don't need a broom, drugs, or any exotic equipment. In a poll taken by *Llewellyn's New Worlds of Mind & Spirit* magazine in 1993, 63 percent of the people answering the poll successfully astral traveled on a regular basis. Most of the remaining 37 percent who said they could not had tried for less than six months. The key is persistence and patience.

Astral travel is no more dangerous for you than driving a car and has some wonderful advantages over working only on the physical plane. It can be a source of comfort to those wanting to contact deceased loved ones or enjoy an astral relationship with both teacher-guides and an astral lover.

The astral planes are a source of unlimited power for working magick, creating manifestations to appear later in your life, or healing yourself and others. You just have to learn how to weave that power into creative strands of energy which you then use to create a thoughtform, powered with the intent which you give it.

In these realms can be found forgotten ancient knowledge, long lost or destroyed here on the physical plane of existence. Through this ancient knowledge you can bring forward ideas for inventions, medical cures, or artistic endeavors. You can view history as it really was, not the rewritten version with which we are acquainted.

While on the astral plane, it is possible for you to take part in ancient sacred ceremonies, learn ancient mystical and spiritual secrets, and be initiated into some of the oldest of Earth's sacred Mystery traditions. You will be allowed to see the Akashic records of your past lives, so you can recognize past mistakes and negative relationships which may be once again causing you trouble.

With the proper attitude and incentive you can expand your spiritual growth, improve your daily life, remove many recurring problems from your existence, and become an all-around better person. The choice to make improvements is yours, just as the effort to accomplish astral travel must be yours.

Hopefully, you are now looking at astral projection and travel with a more positive, realistic view, rather than accepting and believing the old lies about losing your soul, being possessed, or going to hell if you practice it. This type of travel costs you nothing but the effort to do it. The rewards are tremendous. And you don't have to be a witch and ride a broom to get there! Happy journeying.

Glossary

Akashic records: Records kept on the astral plane regarding each human's past lives.

Alpha waves: The borderline brain activity between conscious and subconscious; the creative cycle; 8-13 cycles per second.

Altered state of consciousness: When a person slips from the everyday conscious mind state into the slower cycles of brain-wave activities; the state of mind necessary in order to receive psychic and astral messages.

Astral body: The form humans use to travel through the astral planes; a duplicate of the physical body, but made up of finer vibrations.

Astral dreams: Many humans call their astral travels "dreams," rather than acknowledge them as actual experiences.

Astral energy: The inexhaustible supply of etheric energy found on the astral planes.

Astral entity: Any being or creature which resides on the astral planes and only has an astral form.

Astral planes or levels: The world that interpenetrates and reflects our physical world but operates on a much higher vibrational level.

Astral projection: Projecting the astral body out of its usual position by the physical body and using this form to move about the astral plane or to other physical locations.

Astral travel: Moving about in the astral body while the physical body stays in one place.

Aura: The field of energy around the physical and astral bodies.

Besom: An old name for a broom.

Beta waves: Problem-solving, normal state of conscious brain activity; 13-50 cycles per second.

Bi-location: To be in two locations at one time; when the astral body is seen or felt in one place, while the physical body is busy in another.

Bio-plasma: The aura.

Body-double: The astral body; sometimes the Watcher.

Bune wand: A Scottish name for a broom or riding staff.

Chakras: The seven major light centers in the astral body.

Clairaudience: To hear astrally; to hear astral messages.

Clairvoyance: To see astrally; to see astral entities.

Color therapy: To heal by using certain colors to treat certain illnesses and diseases.

Conscious mind: The left brain; the everyday, ordinary part of the mind we use to logically solve problems.

Controlled projection: Willing oneself to project the astral body away from the physical body; done on command.

Co-walker or *coimimeadh*: A Scottish term for the astral double.

Delta waves: Deep, slow brain activity found in deep sleep; 0.5-3 cycles per second.

Discarnate: An entity without a physical body.

Divination: Using tarot cards, runes, the crystal ball, etc. to look into the future.

Doppelganger: The astral double.

EEG or electro-encephalogram: A machine hooked to the head by little electrodes which record brainwave activity.

Element: The astral-psychic building blocks of all physical and astral matter: Earth, Air, Fire, Water.

Ethereal or etheric: Belonging to the astral.

Ethereal leakage: Energy leakage either from the aura because of damage to it, or energy leaking from the astral into the physical plane.

Etheric double: The astral body.

Fetch: The astral body or double.

Flares: Bursts of energy leaking out of the aura; seen as flares of light.

Flying or magick ointment: The herbal ointment used by medieval witches to cause hallucinations; contained deadly herbs.

Group karma: The karma gathered by a nation or cultural group.

Incarnate: A spirit with a physical body.

Incubus, incubi: Male astral entities, discarnate humans or elementals, who try to engage in sexual activities with humans.

Intuition: The ability to gain knowledge without logical thinking or access.

Karma: The positive and/or negative "debt" gained by actions while in a physical body and carried from one lifetime to another until the "debts" are paid.

Kirlian photography: Special photography which shows the aura surrounding the human body, animals, and plants.

Leannain Sith: A Celtic term for a faery lover.

Left brain: The side of the brain dealing with logic, language, mathematics, etc.

Magick: The taking of energy from the astral planes and, by certain words and actions, weaving it into a desired manifestation on the physical.

Markers: Historical scenes known or discovered during astral travels to help one find the way through time-travel.

Meditation: The quieting of the body and mind in order to establish contact with the astral; used to produce an altered state of consciousness.

Out-of-body experience: Experiences when traveling in the astral body.

Over-look: To know what is occurring in another place by going there astrally or sending the Watcher.

Prana: Astral energy.

Precognition: Knowing something will happen before it does.

Prophecy: To predict future events.

Psychic attack: To be attacked by astral entities, by another human who is astral traveling, or by another human through the use of negative magick.

Psychic centers: The chakras.

Psychic security: Astral forms built to warn you of psychic attack or someone in the astral body snooping on you.

Psychometry: Reading the vibrations of an object in order to discover things about the owner and/or the object's history.

Reincarnation: To return after physical death by birth into another physical body.

Right brain: The side of the brain dealing with intuition, imagination, and creativity.

Scrying: To see into the past or future.

Seachd phaidir: Literally, the seventh prayer, a Scottish term; used in healing.

Second Sight: The ability to see astral entities.

Shadowy body: The Hawaiian term for the astral body.

Silver cord: The connecting line of energy that remains between the physical and astral bodies until death.

Simulacrum: A created thoughtform entity.

Spirit lover: An astral being that has close ties and a relationship with a physical person.

Spontaneous or involuntary projection: Uncontrolled projection of the astral body; usually during an accident, surgery, childbirth, or near-death experience.

Subconscious mind: The right brain; the creative, non-logical side of the mind.

Succubus, succubi: Female astral entities, discarnate humans or elementals, who try to engage in sexual activities with humans.

Superconscious mind: The race mind through which you have connections with everyone who has ever lived.

Sympathetic magick: A physical action during the working of magick that simulates what you want done, such as in poppets, candle burning, etc.

Telekinesis: The moving of an object without physically touching it; this is accomplished with the power of the mind and the astral body.

Telepathy: Sending and receiving messages by the mind.

Terror of the Threshold: The astral entity which guards the boundary between the subconscious and superconscious minds; it takes on the form most feared by the person trying to cross over.

Theta waves: Drowsy state of brain activity; 4-7 cycles per second.

Third eye: The astral "eye"; connected with the brow center in the center of the forehead.

Thoughtforms or Thought-bodies: Astral forms created by intentional and unintentional thoughts; created by strong emotions.

Watcher: An astral thoughtform sent out to observe something or someone while the physical person goes about her/his ordinary activities.

Witchcraft: The Craft; the Wise Ones; a Pagan religion.

Bibliography

Bibb, Benjamin O. and Joseph J. Weed. *Amazing Secrets of Psychic Healing*. West Nyack, NY: Parker Publishing, 1976.

Butler, W. E. *How to Read the Aura, Practice Psychometry, Telepathy & Clairvoyance*. NY: Warner Destiny, 1978.

Carrington, Hereward. *Your Psychic Powers & How to Develop Them*. NY: Newcastle Publishing, 1975.

Cavendish, Richard. *The Black Arts*. NY: G.P. Putnam's Sons, 1967. (Not a book of black magick).

Conway, D. J. *The Ancient & Shining Ones*. St. Paul, MN: Llewellyn Publications, 1993.

Conway, D. J. *By Oak, Ash & Thorn: Modern Celtic Shamanism*. St. Paul, MN: Llewellyn Publications, 1995.

Cunningham, Scott. *The Complete Book of Incense, Oils & Brews*. St. Paul, MN: Llewellyn Publications, 1991.

Cunningham, Scott. *Cunningham's Encyclopedia of Crystal, Gem & Metal Magic*. St. Paul, MN: Llewellyn Publications, 1990.

Cunningham, Scott. *Cunningham's Encyclopedia of Magical Herbs*. St. Paul, MN: Llewellyn Publications, 1985.

214   Cunningham, Scott. *Magical Aromatherapy*. St. Paul, MN: Llewellyn Publications, 1992.

deGivry, Grillot. *Witchcraft, Magic & Alchemy*. NY: Dover, 1971.

de Lys, Claudia. *The Giant Book of Superstitions*. Secaucus, NJ: Citadel Press, 1979.

Denning, Melita and Osborne Phillips. *Astral Projection: The Out-of-Body Experience*. St. Paul, MN: Llewellyn Publications, 1991.

Denning, Melita and Osborne Phillips. *The Development of Psychic Powers*. St. Paul, MN: Llewellyn Publications, 1992.

Duerr, Hans Peter. Trans. Felicitas Goodman. *Dreamtime: Concerning the Boundary Between Wilderness & Civilization*. UK: Basil Blackwell, 1985.

Dumezil, Georges. *Archaic Roman Religion*. 2 vols. Chicago, IL: University of Chicago Press, 1970.

Eliade, Mircea. *Shamanism: Archaic Techniques of Ecstasy*. Princeton, NJ: Princeton University Press, 1964.

Farrar, Janet and Stewart. *The Witches' Way*. UK: Robert Hale, 1984.

Fox, Oliver. *Astral Projection*. New Hyde Park, NY: University Books, 1962.

Frost, Gavin and Yvonne. *The Magic Power of Witchcraft*. West Nyack, NY: Parker Publishing, 1976.

Gerhardi, William A. *Resurrection*. UK: Cassell, 1934.

Glass, Justine. *Witchcraft, The Sixth Sense*. No. Hollywood, CA: Wilshire Books, 1965.

Green, Celia. *Out-of-the-Body Experiences*. UK: Oxford University Press, 1968.

Hazlitt, W. Carew. *Faiths & Folklore of the British Isles*. 2 vols. NY: Benjamin Blom, 1965.

Long, Max Freedom. *The Secret Science Behind Miracles*. Los Angeles, CA: Kosmon Press, 1948.

Flying Without a Broom

Manning, Al G. *The Magic of New Ishtar Power.* West Nyack, NY: Parker Publishing, 1977.

Muldoon, Sylvan and Hereward Carrington. *The Projection of the Astral Body.* York Beach, ME: Samuel Weiser, 1989. (Originally published 1929.)

Norvell, Anthony. *Amazing Secrets of the Mystic East.* West Nyack, NY: Parker Publishing, 1980.

Norvell, Anthony. *The Miracle of Transcendental Meditation.* West Nyack, NY: Parker Publishing, 1972.

Shaw, Indris. *The Sufis.* UK: Octagon Press, 1964.

Spence, Lewis. *The History & Origins of Druidism.* NY: Samuel Weiser, 1971.

Stearn, Jess. *The Power of Alpha-Thinking: Miracle of the Mind.* NY: New American Library, 1976.

Stewart, Louis. *Life Forces: A Contemporary Guide to the Cult & Occult.* NY: Andrews & McMeel, 1980.

Stewart, R. J. *Robert Kirk: Walker Between Worlds. A New Edition of the Secret Commonwealth of Elves, Fauns & Fairies.* UK: Element Books, 1990.

Trigg, Elwood B. *Gypsy Demons & Divinities.* Secaucus, NJ: Citadel Press, 1973.

Turville-Petre, E. O. G. *Myth & Religion of the North.* NY: Holt, Rinehart & Winston, 1964.

Uyldert, Mellie. *The Magic of Precious Stones.* UK: Turnstone Press, 1981.

Valiente, Doreen. *An ABC of Witchcraft Past & Present.* NY: St. Martin's Press, 1973.

Weed, Joseph J. *Wisdom of the Mystic Masters.* West Nyack, NY: Parker Publishing, 1968.

Index